WELLIES AND WARDERS

My Personal Journey

By

Dave Ginnelly

Copyright © Dave Ginnelly 2015

This book is sold subject to the condition that it shall not, by way of trade or otherwise, be lent, resold, hired out, or otherwise circulated without the publisher's prior consent in any form of binding or cover other than that in which it is published and without a similar condition including this condition being imposed on the subsequent publisher.

The moral right of Dave Ginnelly has been asserted.

ISBN-13: 978-1511540179

ISBN-10: 1511540176

DEDICATION

I wish to dedicate the book to my twin brother who died at birth and was not able to take this journey with me.

CONTENTS

CHAPTER 1 1
CHAPTER 2 5
CHAPTER 3 12
CHAPTER 4 21
CHAPTER 5 31
CHAPTER 6 38
CHAPTER 7 46
CHAPTER 8 55
CHAPTER 9 64
CHAPTER 10 73
CHAPTER 11 81
CHAPTER 12 89
CHAPTER 13 97
CHAPTER 14 105
CHAPTER 15 111
CHAPTER 16 120
CHAPTER 17 130
CHAPTER 18 136
CHAPTER 19 145
CHAPTER 20 153
CHAPTER 21 162
CHAPTER 22 171
CHAPTER 23 182
CHAPTER 24 193
CHAPTER 25 204
CHAPTER 26 213
CHAPTER 27 222
CHAPTER 28 230
CHAPTER 29 239
CHAPTER 30 246
CHAPTER 31 255
CHAPTER 32 262

ACKNOWLEDGMENTS

I wish to thank all of these people for their assistance in this project:

Anthony 'ski' Hart

Stephanie Butterick

Jason Ashby

Lisa Ashby

Mark White

Mae Ling

Nick Alcock

Sadie Morgan

Peter Woodward Cregg

Margaret Woodward Cregg

Michael Nesbit (owner of Britain's Gangland Facebook) for producing artwork for cover.

FOREWORD

Could I first point out that this story and the events that take place in it made me the man I am today. It is a very brutal account of my life, and although I feel I owe many people an apology for the violence I meted out, I am sure upon reading further you will appreciate that I also endured excessive brutality too.

It is an account of many years in penal establishments and also two mental institutions.

From being a small boy in a duffle coat and Wellington boots, I would be brutalised from pillar to post for decades.

My story is one of survival and, thankfully, I am still here to tell the story.

Dave Ginnelly, 2015.

CHAPTER 1

I will go into my family background shortly, but for the time being, my father was constantly warning that I was a 'bad little bastard' and that I would soon get my comeuppance when the authorities finally got sick of giving me continual second chances and locked me up at last.

I had just spent a three-day remand at a local boys' Remand Centre and I never appreciated that I was there only for an assessment whilst the courts decided what to actually do with me.

I had entered Tong Park Remand Home in Baildon between Bradford and Leeds, and the boys' ages ranged from perhaps ten to fifteen years of age. Although I had been a little apprehensive upon reaching the home, my fears were quickly allayed by one of the officers in charge of the home asking me politely, "Are you OK? Would you like some more comics to read?"

None of these acts of kindness tallied one bit with the

regular parental warnings of what I could expect, and I soon settled into my new surroundings and could honestly say this was more like a holiday camp than a supposed correctional facility. Considering I was actually eating three meals daily for the first time in my life, to compliment the fact that I also had clean bedding every few days, made me laugh inwardly at the supposed brutality I would be expected to endure whilst being rehabilitated.

Surely my father had been misinformed, because I genuinely felt in the lap of luxury and that life couldn't get much easier to handle than right now! I would be lulled into a false sense of security I would come to regret!

We would be crammed into dormitories of perhaps ten to twelve youngsters, and even this sleeping arrangement was nothing new to me as I had shared a bedroom my whole life.

On regular occasions the member of staff who had either been allocated this particular shift, or on second consideration had actually 'volunteered' for it, would come around checking on the residents, shining his torch around the room. He would be alone and responsible for ensuring that there were no absconders during the night, and this was meant to be the purpose of his visits throughout the night, but I watched interestedly as he coaxed different boys from their beds on the pretext of watching some television as a late-night treat.

Some of the older boys used to giggle, until the night 'security' officer brought the torch down heavily into the small of their backs. When I thought it was safe to talk I asked in a whisper, "What's that all about?" But no one dared speak for fear they could be overheard from the other side of the door.

I was fifteen years old and quickly reassured myself that my age seemed to be of a higher one, thankfully, than was required to earn a late-night 'treat'. Even so, on the three nights I resided in Tong Park I raced each night to grab one of the furthest beds from the door and never fell asleep till I was sure the evening's activities had ceased.

We spent most of the day doing menial work such as polishing and buffing what seemed to me to be a 'home' made completely of mahogany wood. Some of the younger residents were made to bring their sheets down in front of the whole dining room whilst we sat and ate breakfast, and were red-faced and very embarrassed, running to cleanse the urine-stained sheets themselves. They could not have any breakfast until they had done so.

I would cringe for some of these younger boys who would occasionally get a clip around the ear from a member of staff when they ran past, demanding to know when they were going to stop this disgusting activity. Some of the boys would have perhaps been the same ones taken from their beds in the dead of night and I used to watch from a distance, contemplating my own opinions of what I deemed disgusting activity, but already I was mindful of the fact that it would be best for me that I simply keep my head down and remain silent for the duration of my stay.

I wasn't particularly sexually experienced at fifteen years of age, but it didn't take a genius to work out that I mustn't put myself in a situation with one of the officers, who seemed to be renowned for this behaviour, and I managed to keep myself a safe distance from it. Of course I had every sympathy for the boys who it *was* happening to, but already I had begun to learn to adopt a selfish attitude and 'protect yourself' seemed to be the attitude of the other boys.

I had yet to encounter the brutality my father had assured me I would endure, but what I witnessed already in the space of three days certainly made me want to be out of this place at the earliest opportunity.

It was a cold winter morning when the police came to

collect me and transport me to Dewsbury Magistrates in West Yorkshire. It was 1968 and I had finally 'graduated' to the big court as opposed to the juvenile sentencing that I had previously encountered.

I was in court charged with criminal damage at my school, St. John Fishers Roman Catholic School, where I was accused of vandalising my headmaster's office. Of course, I had done it because I had taken exception to the continued corporal punishment I had to endure at the hands of the headmaster, Mr. John Duffy, and simply decided to not only absolutely trash his office, but to snap his 'finely tuned instruments' for the sake of my bruised hands. I will go into more detail later.

But for the present time I was at the mercy of three Magistrates who, after being in a huddle for what seemed like eternity, but more likely was no more than a few minutes, decided I had been given ample opportunity to correct my behaviour, and therefore there was no alternative but to send me to a Detention Centre for three months.

Years later Margaret Thatcher and her cabinet would use crime and punishment as a vote-winner and convince the British public that her government was going to introduce a new sort of regime, were miscreants would be very regimented and made to move 'on-the-double' everywhere. Let me assure every Tory politician from that particular time that the so-called Novel Institution had already long been in existence.

My father's warnings were about to come back, to completely slap me in the face and haunt me!

After a very long journey in handcuffs, I was about to enter the foreboding gates of Kirklevington Detention Centre situated in Yarm, Teesside. This was about to turn very nasty and would give me the biggest wake-up call ever.

CHAPTER 2

I was born David Brian Ginnelly on the 9th December in 1953. Apparently the year of the Coronation, not like I had much to celebrate. I had a sister called Maureen who was a year older than me, and we were brought up by my father, Barry, and my grandmother, Winifred Ginnelly.

My mother had left my father when I was at a very young age. I'd guess about six months old, and I would not get the opportunity to meet my mum for the first time until I was fifteen years old as I will explain later.

We were raised in a very strong Catholic neighbourhood where every single family seemed to have a minimum of ten children, although in reality, maybe not, but there was never any shortage of players when we decided to have a game of street football.

Religion was constantly on the agenda and the very first school I attended, St. Paulinus, in my local area of Westtown, in Dewsbury, taught me that fact at a very early age.

On completion of the register we would find ourselves participating in a full Morning Mass which happened daily in the company of very stern-faced nuns who thought nothing of wrapping a firm cane around the back of one's legs for little or no excuse. This was a school where if silence was called for in the classroom, then SILENCE was instant. It was a very harsh schooling but I can also remember fondly the steam train drivers waving whilst we had our playtimes on the yard.

Most of us in attendance were a right 'rag-tag-and-bobtail' team of waifs and strays who, if we were lucky, had one good pair of shoes and they had to be saved for the once-a-week jaunt to the local Catholic church so that we all looked pristine for the approval of our Maker. In reality, six days out of the week would be spent in Wellington boots, no matter which season of the year it would be at the time. More often than not, it would be without the accompaniment of socks. I lost count of the times I would cry myself to sleep with the sore circles on my shins and calves where the rubber material had chafed my skin, but it would 'toughen me up and make me a man', I would be told often.

Not even the slightest hint of a tub of Sudocrem or the appropriate cream of the time was proffered, but I suppose I had to resign myself to the fact that I would at least become a man quicker than the other children.

Times were very hard and I quickly realised never to ask for or crave anything because it would never be forthcoming, although I also realised my grandmother always seemed to have funds to go to the local bingo hall, or my father the local betting shops, Dewsbury Celtic Working Men's Club, or other various social clubs. My grandmother would take me with her at all times when she went to the bingo and would always have a very large bag of Mint Imperial sweets in her pocket. To this day I am still not sure if they were her favourites or if they were simply to keep me quiet.

There were very few home comforts, and certainly no carpets on the floor. In the kitchen stood a great barrel which sat below the mangle, and I would stand and watch my grandma wash any amount of clothes in the kitchen sink and then run them through the mangle to squeeze the excess water from them. It seemed as if we had it all, to a young boy's eyes, albeit I hadn't visited any of my friends' homes at that time to realise that we were nowhere near having the appliances of the time. By the time Grandma had completed her chores the clothes would be reasonably dry, although every button on every shirt would be broken in half or hanging by a thread.

I must have looked a sorry state each time I attended school, but I would get the opportunity to have a meal and even drink free milk that was provided, although on several occasions I would be asked to tell the teacher that I wasn't particularly thirsty and would it be possible for me to take mine home to consume, only to find that I would lose it to Father's or Grandma's tea.

A lot of the women on the estate used to work in the local rag warehouses, and their job would entail cutting all the zips away from old clothes and placing them in cotton or woollen receptacles. A latter day form of recycling, but one of the 'perks' of the job was that the women could take home certain items of clothing should they think they may come in handy for their own or other families to wear. Needless to say I used to end up amassing lots of these clothes, and I would cry that I had to attend school in these musky-smelling clothes because, without doubt, all the other children would be looking in my direction more often than not.

The only day that seemed to be of significance to any parent at all would be each Sunday, when you would have to look twice to confirm that, yes indeed, it was your best friend from school, except for the fact he was dressed like an Eton choirboy. If anyone in the community didn't attend church then the priest would be at that person's door during the week demanding an explanation.

My grandma used to take what she thought was the easy option and send some money with me for the offertory box, because she thought paying a penance would absolve her non-attendance in the eyes of the Lord, but more often than not it was a 60/40 split and most definitely not in favour of the church roof.

Religion was just drilled into us over and over, and yes, at times I feared the consequences of stealing from the church, but any 'higher being' looking down would have seen how hypocritical the majority of the estate were, and it was only the odd sixpence I was purloining – not exactly a king's ransom considering the hardship I constantly endured.

The time fast approached when I was due to sit my exams for my 11-Plus to determine which secondary school I was to attend, and I was expected to pass with flying colours for inclusion to the grammar school, which was four miles away in Wakefield. But upon listening to regular shouting matches between my father and Grandma about the additional costs, I decided to do the honourable thing and fail my exams dismally. It came as a great surprise to my teachers and they wished me a sad farewell to the regular secondary modern, St. John Fishers, which was practically on my doorstep.

Already at the early age of eleven years I had learnt the valuable lesson that being poor can be very much a hindrance.

Now even though I had failed intentionally, and perhaps my father should have realised this and assisted me more with my new school, I found myself being called out of assembly each and every day, along with my sister, for not having the correct uniform on. This would result in me having to place each hand out to receive corporal punishment, as each Monday morning came around and I was still in non-uniform.

I resented my father because I had witnessed him out drinking each weekend even though there were no funds for the purchase of a uniform. But I resented this headmaster even more for bruising my hands to the extent that he did.

It soon followed that I became a long-term truant and I was getting no education at all. I would spend my days in derelict properties, lighting fires to keep warm and just idling the days away. I had developed a hatred for all within the educational system and I felt let-down because deep down in my heart I knew I was a bright individual, and I hadn't even been given a chance, so I decided to target the teachers who had isolated me from their classes by making me stand in the corridors.

Within a short distance from the school, on a route that the teachers passed, lay a maternity ward which had a pear orchard surrounded by a high wall that I would perch myself on top of with a choice selection of the most putrid pears which had long since fallen from the trees. As each teacher passed by I shouted to get their attention and make them look up. Needless to say I messed up a lot of faces whilst listening to their barrage of abuse.

By now my absence from school had attracted the attention of the legal protocol brigade and my father received summons after summons from the court, and an agreement was reached that Social Services would provide me with adequate schoolwear and I would return to school at the earliest opportunity, or my father would incur very heavy financial fines.

So off I went for my re-introduction to school looking prettier than a choirboy, but the battle lines had already been drawn, and I wasn't the most popular pupil. I felt I was getting disciplined far more than any other pupil, and if they wanted a rebel, then I would give them exactly what they wanted.

By now I had taken to tattooing myself with India ink and needles tied together with cotton, and although I had managed to hide them sufficiently under the sleeves of my shirt I had come to the decision to shock the whole system, so I had tattooed a cross very prominently onto my chin. The stir this caused in the assembly hall the next Monday morning started with a slow murmur and whisper, and elbow after elbow nudging each other until all this was interrupted by a thunderous roar from the headmaster as he commanded me to go to his office immediately.

Once again, for perhaps the hundredth time, I waited outside his office in the knowledge that there was only going to be one outcome. Should I let this man domineer me as he had done for years? The look on his face was priceless when I refused to hold out my hand and informed him I wasn't going to accept it anymore.

Whatever composure he should have had as principal of a school went completely out of the window as he proceeded to attempt to whip me around the legs. I grabbed his cane on the downward stroke and snapped it in front of him, and promised him faithfully he would never be doing that to me again, while running down the corridor and out of the school.

I sat on the wall of the orchard to assess the consequences of my actions, and it was crystal clear that my days of schooling were over, but I most certainly didn't dare go home yet to face my father's wrath.

My anger hadn't lessened any, and once darkness fell I doubled back to the school and proceeded to smash each window of the headmaster's office, and eventually climbed through. It was like I was letting years and years of frustration out, making sure along the way to snap every single cane in his collection.

Not even one poor soul would be getting any corporal punishment in the morning, but would my own punishment befit the crime?

CHAPTER 3

I had never heard of Kirklevington Detention Centre or of its location in Teesside, but I was about to learn a whole lot more.

"Get out of that fucking van! You little bastard," shouted the first guard, who greeted me by throwing me up the wall and insisting I learn every one of the rules and regulations by the time that he returned, which wasn't going to be long considering he only had to complete the formalities of signing me into his custody.

The police officers who had transported me must have done this same journey on countless occasions, and had warned me regularly throughout the journey that I was about to lose the chip on my shoulder. My response would be to smirk, but even this soon into the reception area, with the taste of blood in my mouth as a result of being thrown against the wall, I knew I had certainly underestimated the situation I was in and I would need to remain alert.

The two police officers would need to cover the same distance to get back home so they were in no mood to hang about exchanging pleasantries, although you could maybe sense that were they given the opportunity to have ringside seats to witness my imminent introduction to this very physically taxing regime, they would relish it, but it was off to a calmer environment for them.

Fortunately I wasn't asked, but I doubt if I could have memorised even one rule or regulation by the time the warder returned. My mind was racing as he screamed at me to jump into what turned out to be a very cold bath indeed. I thought about reminding him that it was the middle of winter but intuition told me that for the next three months, I wouldn't be questioning anything.

I had shoulder length hair at this time, which I was pulled out of the bath by and assured that I would be losing by the morning. It mattered little that I was about to lose my hair. Keep it by all means kind sir, but the loss of my freedom now gave me greater concern. I was ordered to put on some very ill-fitting clothes and pick up a rolled bundle which consisted of everything I would need in this hell hole. I was instructed to sign all of my personal belongings into prison property, and I would receive them back in eight weeks' time as the warder explained to me that I only had to serve eight weeks, as I would be given four weeks off automatically.

This came as a great relief to me and, as if sensing my smugness, the officer informed me that I would be on my knees begging to leave after eight weeks, and I'd no reason to doubt his threatening warning. His manner as he spoke to another officer who had come to collect me seemed to have softened, as they discussed everyday topics like the weather or football results, and for that brief moment I relaxed and leaned up against the wall.

A right hand landed and took me clean off my feet as he barked at me to pick up my things and run along this corridor, and stop at a certain fire extinguisher on the wall. By now the realisation had finally set in that, choose the wrong fire extinguisher to stop at, and yet again you are about to be given a single punch or a combination, depending on how sadistic this bastard is, who revels in beating adolescents that haven't even left school yet.

Even to this day it is described as 'short, sharp shock' treatment and in more cases than not it deters offenders from ever committing crime again. Unfortunately it didn't work for me, as you will find out in later chapters.

For a start, who is going to complain about the brutality and, more to the point, who is going to listen? You have parents who are at their wits end regarding the behaviour of unruly children, and if this sort of brutality corrects that behaviour, then you won't find too many in disagreement with whatever untoward tactics are used. This place was crazy and completely run on a disciplinary principle, with lots of orders and everything done with military precision.

I was shown to my cell downstairs and locked in for the evening, with the warning to get in my bed early as I would need my rest. I had never been more relieved to hear a cell door shut in my whole life, safe in the knowledge I wouldn't be encountering any more physical assaults for the time being.

I awoke with a start to the sound of a big bell chiming away and immediately thought, *Christ's sake! What fucking time is it?* Upon looking out of my window I witnessed lots of youngish boys sprinting out onto what turned out to be a large drill yard. They had small shorts and sleeveless-type vests, and as I watch carefully they began to do star jumps, press-ups, and other physical exercises in a very regimented manner. It was like observing synchronised swimming or something similar, as everyone seemed in perfect unison with each other. I continued watching, thinking these lads must have really been misbehaving to have to endure this sort of physical torture at this ungodly hour, when suddenly my cell door was thrown open and I had to listen to a torrent of abuse as to why the fuck I didn't have my P.E. kit on, and was told to "Move it NOW – ON THE DOUBLE!"

I'd barely opened my eyes and already the day had begun exactly how the night ended up. A firm punch to the side of my head followed this time, with a sharp follow-up to my stomach which completely winded me and sent me to the floor, wheezing.

While this happened all the other boys on my landing were running past, giggling to themselves, dressed in the same attire as the other boys I had seen in the yard shortly before. This same situation would have befallen them in previous weeks, when they had at one time been the new kids on the block. The greenhorn. Unfamiliar with what was expected. I was to repeat this scenario myself in the coming weeks, but for the meantime I was more than a little scared.

I unravelled the kit I had been given the previous night in what must have been near record time, and ran along a long corridor and out into the foreboding yard, dressed in the exact same style as my other co-inhabitants. Whilst running along the corridor I was able to observe by the large clock on the wall in the dining hall that it was in actual fact only six o'clock in the morning. *Are these people mental?* I thought to myself, but within seconds of reaching the drill yard I was instantly jumping as one with the rest of the lads. I thought my lungs would burst as I was shouted at by different officers at intervals to 'STEP IT UP' or some other criticism about my timing being out. I couldn't take it all in and was terrified that I was going to collapse on the spot.

Occasionally, when the officers were out of earshot,

one of the other boys would ask which area of the country you were from. I enquired as to how long this went on for and was informed it was just to loosen us up before breakfast at 7 a.m. Although this news gave me comfort at the time, I was quickly to realise it was simply the beginning of a long and arduous day which culminated in falling into your bed each night completely exhausted and too tired to even think.

After breakfast, which I devoured like a starving wolf, I was allocated another inmate to teach me exactly how to lay my kit out on my bed. This involved your pyjamas being folded exactly four stripes wide and then the edge of them being lightly tapped by a nail brush until a crease developed, thereby giving the end result of a perfectly shaped box.

Once this first task was complete each and every other article of clothing was required to be folded to the exact size of the pyjamas and in the same manner, with the accompanying crease. I joked to the recently acquired friend that it was akin to being in the army. He took me to a window, where it was possible to see an army-like assault course, which he told me we had to complete each and every day, and the only reason we weren't doing it now was because it was my induction day and I needed to be trained up first in the exacting task of folding this kit up.

It transpired that 'Steve' only had a matter of days left, and being as how he was almost at the end of his sentence, he had been allocated lighter duties such as training up the inmates.

We spent the rest of the morning preparing a full kit for inspection, then pulling it all apart and time after time repeating the procedure until he felt I had mastered it. On the odd occasion I felt he was maybe being a bit too particular, he took me to look through the spy hole into the other lads' cells and I was amazed how pristine and perfect everything seemed. He assured me that upon inspection by any one of the officers in charge of our cell block, should even one item be out, even by a fraction, the whole bed would be tipped upside down, so I quickly picked up any tips he wished to pass on.

'Steve' was a friendly lad, but he could only help me for the one day, as the following day he would be doing the exact same routine with the previous night's latest arrival.

I grasped as much information as I could, and he told me I would be monitored carefully on all of the physical activities, albeit only for the first few weeks, because after that interim period the officers would re-focus on prisoners who had arrived after I had. Seemed simple! I just had to convince the officers that I was now fit enough not to warrant their constant attention and it would give me the opportunity to take a few shortcuts.

I had got the hand of laying out a kit for inspection by the time lunchtime came around and made my way to the dining hall to be fed. I was hungry, but still felt so apprehensive and nervous and failed to finish my meal. I was more interested in looking around to see if any faces were familiar, but there was no one I knew. I quickly noticed how fit and healthy the majority of them looked, but I was soon to find out the contributory factor to their well being and athleticism.

I was placed in my cell immediately after dinner and told it would be opened again in an hour's time, so rather than waste my time I once again practiced my kit layout and I was more than impressed with what I'd learned in the morning and after all, I had managed to reach lunch without being struck about the head even once, told me I must be doing something right, but inwardly I'd already also thought 'no way will I let these bastards intimidate me'.

In the afternoon I was taken to the yard along with six others and for hour upon hour we were taught how to march round and round. 'Attention' or 'stand easy'. 'Right wheel, left wheel, about turn'. I found it all quite amusing, although I never let either of the officers see this or I would most certainly be getting the next punch I had been so happy to avoid.

We were also shown how to fasten up ankle gaiters and polishing of boots, including the underside of the boots. This was definitely an institution not lacking in cleanliness and order and it resembled army barracks more by the day. So in the blink of an eye I had now mastered the art of passing a kit inspection, marching and polishing and the most important lesson of all, which was when that bell rings early morning be out of that bed and running on the spot by the time the door opens.

I soon made some new friends and when the opportunity arose we joked our way through the day. These moments were few and far between, so when they came, needed embracing like a new born baby.

Days soon ran into weeks and I became so much fitter in myself and must have begun to impress because I would be able to skip the odd exercise on the white-knuckle ride that was the assault course. This course would put any regular army circuit to shame and we were expected to complete four laps. I found a lot of exercises within my reach except the spider's web consisting of ropes extending thirty feet up, as I had always had a problem with heights, and so after scaling halfway up would duck through the side and it would appear I had reached the summit and was now coming down the other side.

This place was a strictly no smoking institution and within no time my health and fitness were now very finely tuned. It was maybe cruel of us to laugh and mock the new arrivals, but we ourselves at one point of our incarceration had been made fun of in the self same way.

Everything seemed based around circuit training indoors in the gymnasium or the feared outdoor assault course in simply P.E. vests, shorts and the obligatory work boots which amassed layers of mud by the time I'd be completing my fourth lap. When we weren't in the gym we would be called on to labour at the interior farm and this involved, in the main, picking and sorting vegetables or sawing railway sleepers into blocks and then chopping into firewood sticks for the local pensioners. We had lots of laughs and relaxed considerably down on the farm unless certain officers with a sadistic nature were responsible for us and they would bring out the dreaded 'ARROW'

The 'Arrow' consisted of the plough that is connected by chains and a bar to shire horses to work up and down fields. Six of us were made to pull the bar up and down a very steep incline whilst the officer would place a railway sleeper on top of the spikes, then stand upon it himself ensuring the soil was deeply ploughed. From his vantage point he could also observe our knuckles and assess who was pulling or who was shirking and you would feel the force of his stick firmly on the back of your hands. Brutal, but effective.

It was this sort of manual labour that made me realise I wasn't cut out to be a shire horse and I settled for the easier option of furthering my education which I had been told about by a friend. I don't know why I'd waited so long to apply. Maybe I still had a strong aversion to anything educational, but upon attending my fist class and being able to witness the exertions of the farm labourers from the confines of the classroom window, then no more consideration was needed. The gentle manner of the female tutor assured me I had made the right choice.

Instantly, I sensed her sympathetic attitude towards how we were being harshly treated and I kicked myself for waiting four weeks to opt for the classroom. It was the best attended school in existence and although some officers knew we were playing the system, the bottom line was, the majority of us had been lacking in schooling for many years.

So the time came when it was the day of my discharge, and although they may have felt they had instilled a more gentlemanly approach to my attitude I was about to turn that idea right on its head. Apparently, I was to be escorted to the Eaglescliffe train station and from there to York via Darlington and finally from York to Leeds. I had been informed that the officer in charge of my escort was to remain with me at Eaglescliffe station until the train pulled off from the station, because until that moment I was officially still in the custody of the detention centre and I was about to be given the opportunity to even give a little payback for all of the brutality I had endured the past eight weeks. This was gilt edged and would also let at least one of the bastards know that here's one person whose spirit you hadn't broken.

I hurried quickly to the buffet cart and snatched up the first available empty plastic cup I could find and proceeded to the toilet. I'd never been as excited about urinating for a long time and filled the cup to overflowing. I hastened to the window, fearful that if the train pulled off the opportunity would be gone. The officer exchanged pleasantries whilst standing on the platform wishing me well for the future. Obviously oblivious to the fact that, to my knowledge, he had punched me on two occasions. The train went to pull out and as the officer turned away, confident his duties were done, I shouted to attract his attention and when he looked back, let him have a full cup of urine all over him and in my own inimitable way, wished him well for the future.

God forbid I ever find myself in that same institution again or I would maybe have found myself buried down the farm.

CHAPTER 4

I don't think I had intentionally set out to be a 'bad bastard' as my father called me on regular occasions. Life just didn't seem to be as fortunate to me as others around me, it seemed, and I began to take a few wrong turns, resulting in being placed on probation at a very early age.

I had been caught shoplifting on a few foolhardy expeditions to the local town centre, when perhaps I should have attempted this on days when the shops were crowded with other children. Most certainly not on a day when I was absent from my school and I wouldn't exactly have been the best dressed truant in the shop or store. I may as well have had a big sign saying 'I'm a skint horrah urchin and if you watch me carefully you will soon witness me stealing'.

It was too late now for any regrets, but the realisation that I wasn't a very good shoplifter made me make an alternative career choice, as I wasn't about to conform as my precious little probation officer seemed to think, and overnight I became an office burglar.

I'd been involved in petty theft for a while now, and from once being in popular demand as a babysitter on my local estate, the offers soon dried up. I'd been able to bluff it for a while as I had found a way of accessing the pre-payment on the hired television sets and I used to take the contents, regularly consisting of pre-decimal sixpences and shillings, and would regularly have large pocketfuls of loose change. I had even done the same in my own family home, which proved to be fortunate because on one occasion my grandma had remarked, whilst putting in a coin, that it sounded empty to her. It made me realise that perhaps similar suspicions may have arisen in other households. I needed to act quickly or my newfound source of income would soon come to a sticky end.

I gathered together an assortment of washers, nails, or anything with metal content which would act as a decoy within the payment boxes, and then set about re-opening each box once the opportunity arose. Once I had opened each box I then placed the aforementioned items within, closed the box, and inserted a coin using the regular procedure until I was satisfied that the coin making contact with the other objects made the required sound of metal on metal, so the suspicions would be allayed, if only for the time being.

Of course I retrieved my coin that I'd used for the trial. Why not? I'd already made my bed and these matters were going to come to light sooner rather than later, so it was simply a case of 'in for a penny – in for a pound' and I would face the consequences as and when.

It all may seem a little bit out of order but one or two households had used me in a babysitting capacity on numerous occasions and had conveniently forgotten to pay me or simply duped me by promising double pay the following week, which never materialised, and my patience had worn a little thin – perhaps this cleared my conscience a little.

Of course I understood we all lived in a poor environment and money was tight throughout the neighbourhood, but the same destitution reigned in my home too. At least the homes where I had been caring for the children seemed to be a little more presentable than my own home. It wasn't as if these people were sitting in a tin bath in front of a coal fire and having to struggle constantly, but again, I may be looking for reasons to condone my activities.

Obviously it wouldn't be much longer, and my childminding positions would be very limited once the proverbial 'shit hit the fan', but I really didn't care by that point. I used to laugh away to myself often, and would have paid a king's ransom to be in attendance when the recipient of the contents of the boxes emptied it onto the floor for what was usually the quarterly take and rebate to the householder... or so I thought!

The day must have come when my own home had been visited and throughout the day my grandma had given no indication of what had taken place regarding the visit by the custodian of the meter. Had she had told me, I would have made myself very scarce indeed. It wouldn't have made much sense being in the vicinity once my father had been informed of my untoward actions.

Foolishly I had remained in the home, and never once realised Grandma seemed to be taking longer than usual in preparing the family meal. I had usually eaten mine and would be off on my adventures by the time my father was home from work and sitting down to his own meal. This time I was sat at the table without a care in the world, eating away, but out of the corner of my eye I could see on the threshold of our two-bedroomed flat that my grandma was in a huddle, whispering away to my father.

Alarm bells began to ring and I quietly placed my cutlery down, knowing full well the opportunity to complete my meal to its full satisfaction was about to vanish before my eyes. In the blink of an eye my father had me by the throat and dragged me into the living room. He almost knocked the television over in his haste to practically squeeze my face into the root of my present predicament – the dreaded box. He demanded an explanation and none was forthcoming, although inwardly I was disappointed that I had spent all my formative years clad in Wellington boots and hand-me-down clothes, but in my heart I knew it would be futile to inflame the present situation.

I took a few blows, as I had done on many occasions before, accepting I had perhaps merited them on this occasion, but I was fast approaching the time when I would not have to live in this home much longer. I was not happy and had lots of dreams and visions for my future, even though I had barely hit my teens.

I was made to stand on my tiptoes up against the wall, but at least it gave me respite from the rest of the physical beating which would be on the horizon shortly, and without daring to look around I could hear my grandma's pleadings with my father to not be so brutal with me. I knew, as always, this would fall on deaf ears.

It had reached breaking point for me, and I resolved to no longer accept this situation and to run away at the earliest opportunity. I agree readily that I was becoming a bit of a problem child but in my own mind I simply felt that my state of poverty could have been improved at any time, but they had chosen not to, and I craved what other children had. On regular occasions I would stand with my face pressed up to the local fish shop window, dressed like some Victorian urchin, until one of the female counter assistants would beckon me in while the proprietor was busy elsewhere. She would place her finger to her mouth, indicating for me to remain silent as she ruffled my hair, but she need not worry as I would be too busy gorging myself on the proffered repast.

There had to be more to life than this. I was sick to the back teeth of people showing me pity, as I always seemed to be roaming the estate hungry and unkempt. Indoors at my home it seemed like we lived in a bygone age. There was not even the resemblance of a cooker. There was one gas ring on the hob that was more akin to an experimental item from a school science lab. On the rare occasions that we had a full meal items would be warmed up one at a time. More often than not meals would consist of tripe, onions and vinegar, or slices of bread and dripping. God knows what present day dieticians would make of it. It certainly didn't represent a balanced diet for a growing lad.

I had made my mind up. Enough was enough, and once my father had banished me upstairs I instantly knew that my beating would continue at a later stage of the evening, but on this occasion the outcome would be much different.

I opened the bedroom window and gingerly reached out until my hand secured contact with the far from stable cast iron drainpipe. I felt uneasy as I swung my other hand out to gain the comfort of the dual-hand contact, but I was there! I had made it!

There was no going back now as I shinned myself down three floors till I reached the safety of the ground floor. I drifted around aimlessly for the rest of the night until the mass collection of what we called 'chumps' caught my eye. 'Chumps' was the huge assembly of all things wooden and other odds-and-ends gathered together for the up and coming celebration of lighting the annual bonfire for Guy Fawkes Night.

Now most children of the day had a good sense of adventure, and within the structure of the bonfire would be a secret den, which mainly consisted of someone's three-piece suite and I inched my way inside until I found exactly that and made myself 'at home'.

I could feel what I imagined to be fleas and various other insects jumping around my new abode. I could make out the revelling voices of people on their way home after an evening at the local pub or club. I lay there, scared for a while. What if one of these rowdy drunkards took it on themselves to commit an arson attack on my newfound home? But eventually my fatigue got the better of me and I drifted off into a very deep sleep.

I awoke rather cold and most certainly hungry, and I had also accumulated one or two bites about my body. My adventure and visions of a better future had not got off to the best of starts, but at least my destiny was in my own hands. Brighter futures could wait for a later date. Much higher on the agenda was my severe hunger pains. I had not even completed my previous evening's meal due to my father's wrath. I had no shame because lots of people throughout the estate knew of my hardy existence. Therefore I set about simply asking people outright for money on the pretext that my grandma was not at home. Even though they perhaps knew I was feeding them a 'cock-and-bull' story they gave me the odd few coppers regardless. The little money I had managed to beg was barely enough to get me through the day, but at least I did not have to go home with my tail between my legs which, at my lowest point, I had been considering doing.

Obviously by now I would like to think they would be concerned for my safety and well-being, but perhaps not. Anyway, I was determined to prove my point by staying away, standing on my own two feet. I needed additional funds, so I entered the local newsagents where at one time I had been employed as a newspaper delivery boy, and I engaged the owner in conversation. He seemed happy enough chatting and said I was helping his day pass more quickly. Little did he know that I was waiting for that one moment when he was preoccupied, and I snatched as many packets of cigarettes as I could in that instant and made for the door, all the time aware of him screaming expletives at me. But I was gone in an instant.

I loitered outside the local pub and sold my ill-gotten wares at a cheap rate. Not that it mattered to them where I had purloined these items from. It would mean they had the price of an additional pint or two in their pockets. So everyone's a winner!

My hand-to-mouth existence persisted for a further three days and nights, but by now I was looking the worse for wear, especially as the previous night's downfall of rain had breached my linoleum homemade defence, and I was a little bit cold and damp to say the least.

One of the more kindly neighbours who had encountered me in my bedraggled state invited me in and made me a warm meal and a hot drink. She did not want to get involved on a personal level but advised me I could not keep living the way I was, and made me aware of what was called 'The Cruelty Man'. I now know this person to be a representative of the local N.S.P.C.C., which was perhaps the social services of the time.

Although I was growing into a strong-willed person I knew my situation was becoming impossible to maintain and so, with a reluctant heart, I went to the local phone kiosk and having spoken to the concerned parties I arranged to meet at my favourite landmark, the chippy.

When the man showed up he didn't need to look very far to identify who his supposed victim was. I must have looked a very sad and sorry state as I begged him to take me away to a children's home.

He sat and reasoned with me and listened intently to all I had to say – I must have looked a right little hobo in my dishevelled state. I'd not even been close to soap or water for the past three days. Obviously I coloured the details a little and left out the fact that I was not just a 'bad bastard' but recently I had become a thieving one at that. I could have told him the whole truth and the outcome would still have been the same, because the principles of the man's profession meant that he disagreed with any physical brutality to any child, no matter what that child's misdemeanours were.

I quickly gathered that I had gained a sympathetic ear, and milked it to the maximum, telling him tale after tale of abuse, believing I was talking my way, by the minute, into what I believed to be the comfort of a local children's home. Little did I know that a certain procedure had to be followed and the initial process simply entailed us all discussing amongst ourselves, including my father, any possible outcome.

He had listened to me at great length in the comfort of his car, and although I told him I was fearful of ever going back in the family home for even a single moment, his assurances that I would not encounter any more violence allayed my fears.

When we arrived my grandma threw her arms around me and I could sense her relief that I had come to no harm. My Gran loved me. Bless her! She had spent many a year protecting me from any undeserved clip around the face, although even she realised this time that I had overstepped the mark with recent thefts. The man set about warning my father in great detail of the dire consequences of his actions, and the possible outcome should it happen again, and although looking back they in fact were the 'victims', the 'Cruelty Man's lecture had swung the situation back in my favour – for the time being I felt untouchable.

A decision was made that I was to remain at home, albeit with no further physical chastisement, and an uneasy truce was reached. The man departed, assuring me that should I feel threatened in any shape or form, he could be contacted at his local offices. Now of course it is right and proper that these organisations exist for those situations that are possibly much more serious than my own, but I had now found myself in such a lawless state of ill-discipline that I felt I no longer had to obey any rules of life.

It seemed I could do whatever I liked without chastisement, and I did exactly that for the next however many months. I could see lots of things I was doing would have my father inwardly seething but fearful of any repercussions should he hit me. It was as if I had placed him in handcuffs.

I never stole from my family again because even I had begun to appreciate that the actions I had taken had placed them in even deeper debt. The money I had stolen had to be paid back by them over a period of time. I should never have placed them in that position. They did love me and my father worked hard, and I now fully understand those principles. But I was young and wanted it all, and began roaming around the estate stealing anything and everything, safe in the knowledge that the most I would endure would be a verbal reprimand, and I could handle that quite easily.

I became more and more out of control. Schooling went out of the window and on the rare occasions that I actually attended it would be to agitate and be disruptive. The lack of discipline at home must have rubbed off on my sister, Maureen, because out of the blue she was whisked away to some sort of home for naughty girls, and it would be many years before I would see her again. Something had to give, because I was spiralling towards disaster. This was now a runaway train which could crash at any time. Whilst I walked the estate many of the neighbours would look at me with disgust, and I was relishing in the fact that I could do whatever I liked and no one could prevent me.

I was like a house of cards waiting to collapse, and I

had now come to the attention of the local police, who were quite happy for me to dig my own grave with my behaviour. The collapse of my 'cards' eventually came by way of me thinking that, due to there being no discipline at home, I could pull off the same routine at my school, culminating in my aforementioned destruction of my headmaster's office.

I was not only in the sights of the local police. I had placed my head above the trenches and with it I had gained what turned out to be a very long and disastrous criminal record. With that first sentence my demise had begun!

CHAPTER 5

The train pulled away from the Eaglescliffe station and I was in hysterics with the manner in which my cupful of urine had managed to hit the officer exactly the way I'd intended.

So I'd completed my first sentence and finished it on a high note, and anyone who thought that this 'bad bastard' had lost the chip on his shoulder better think again. I had met lots of boys in Kirklevington Remand Centre, we all ranged from between fourteen and sixteen years old, and many of them were much more clued-up in the wicked ways of the world than I could possibly be. I was only from a reasonably sized town, whereas some of these lads where born and bred city boys, and had a much better understanding of crime than I ever thought possible, and I had learnt just as much about easier ways to profit from crime as the disciplinarian regime presumed they had taught me about authority.

I came out of there fitter than I would ever be my whole life through. I had only ever been a quite skinny boy but the regime I had just left had given me a very muscular, toned physique and I most certainly had a very good spring in my step.

I should have maintained the same sort of discipline for my own personal gain but that rebellious streak, knowing you are no longer having to conform to a strict regime, soon sends that thought out of the window, and at the first opportunity I bought a packet of cigarettes, and so, within hours of being discharged, already the last eight weeks spent acquiring a good level of fitness was being challenged.

Being able to suddenly obtain everything that I had not been allowed for the past few months just happened naturally, and within no time at all it was as if I had never been away and I fell back into a familiar pattern.

My reputation on the estate preceded me. Every man and his dog was aware of the fact that I had been away and locked up. Not before time, a lot of them would have been thinking, as I ambled through the neighbourhood, feeling perhaps a little sheepish. I hadn't managed to have even one visit whilst I had been away, and therefore had not seen my family in the past few months, and I was greeted warmly, like the prodigal son returning. My father had even taken the day off work to welcome me home, which he could ill-afford to do, and I had never felt this amount of love before within this household. I now became a little embarrassed at the stigma I had placed on them. They had done nothing wrong and I was the one that had inflicted all of this shame on them when they were blameless, really. I decided in that instant that I would make an almighty attempt to try and turn my life around and redirect myself. It was the least they could expect.

Not a lot had changed. Our home was still very sparsely furnished and on each occasion I ate I would have to sit on the floor to consume it. My father was constantly in gainful employment and yet money was always in short supply with respect to home comforts, and I promised myself faithfully that for any home that I should have in the future, I would make every effort to make that home comfortable and lacking in nothing.

The rumour must have spread like a bush fire that I had been released and it did not take long to come to the attention of my school, who must have wasted no time whatsoever in contacting the local education authority. I was notified at the earliest opportunity that I would not be expected to be in attendance now or at any other time, and the inference was that due to my continued bad behaviour, there was no other school prepared to take me on, giving due consideration to the fact that I only had a matter of months left anyway. So this decision seemed to determine my next move and took the matter out of my hands.

I could understand the school's decision because, had I been allowed to attend, I would have been greeted like a hero, even for only temporarily abolishing capital punishment by way of me destroying the collection of canes.

I would not have wanted any more trouble for now because I had promised I would improve my behaviour. All of the other youths about to leave school would be discussing their careers with a 'job officer' but I would not be afforded that opportunity. But I didn't care. It mattered nothing to me who would like to be a train driver, fireman or nurse. It all seemed comical to me.

If I thought I was just going to idle the days away I had another thing coming as my father had spoken to his employer of the day. A cotton mill in Hopton, Mirfield, West Yorkshire, and before I could say 'not sure I want to work there' I found myself working forty hours a week in the mill, all for the princely sum of £6/5s pre-decimal, which I can assure you was practically nothing.

I was to stand at a loom picking up any loose ends and threading them back together and would be on my feet all day long, walking backwards and forwards, and mills had not changed much at that time from the previous century. Even with respect to my age the situation may have been slightly illegal as I had acquired the actual job whilst I should still have been in education, but when had that ever been a problem with mill owners in times gone by? I think the job had been created more as a favour to my father, who had worked there for quite a few years.

Unfortunately he may have had to relay a little more background about myself than maybe he should have; the gossip quickly filtered down to the shop floor that I had been recently released from a penal institution and within no time I sensed a lot of the workforce had chosen to shun me in one way or another. I soon gathered that people can be very judgemental and got accustomed to the fact that certain individuals preferred not to converse with me.

I chose not to tell my father and instead led him to believe I was content in my place of work. It was rather the opposite and I quickly became disillusioned with the whole setting, and would spend long lonely days by myself for long periods. I would occasionally pass the point where my father would be playing cards on his lunch break. I would always smile and give him the impression that his son was happy in the ways of the world.

I had only been employed a matter of months when my father was suddenly taken ill and had a spell in Dewsbury General Hospital, and I was given the task of informing the appropriate bodies at work. They were genuine in their sentiment and wished my father well, and I relayed these thoughts to my grandma. But overnight my situation took a turn for the worse. I was not being paranoid. I had been tolerated simply because of my father's good standing and their respect for him, but now the goal posts had moved!

I was ignored blatantly and given harder and harder

tasks to complete. The seeds had been sown and I was to be pushed out of the door. I could do nothing right and was criticised constantly. The final insult came when I asked about the possibility of having a meal at the works canteen and paying for it the following day when I had received my weekly wage, but was told that this couldn't be permitted. It was no more than I'd been allowed to do on several previous occasions. The canteen staff assured me it was now to be the same principle for everyone, but I doubted this.

Although my father had put his reputation on the line for me, he was not aware of the witch-hunt against me and I stormed out of the premises in a blind rage. I spent the rest of the day wasting the hours away and arrived home at the usual time, giving the impression I had completed my shift and all was well in the world.

I was incensed by the way I had been treated and foolishly came to the rash decision to return and burgle the premises that same night. Bearing in mind that I would need funds if I wanted to keep up the pretence that I was still attending my place of work.

No doubt there would have been more money in the admin office, but on occasions in the past I had innocently observed where not only the canteen money was stored, but also the football coupon for the pools, as well as money for an upcoming works outing to the coast.

I placed my coat over the window pane to muffle the noise and tapped a largish stone against the glass until it broke. I then removed all of the loose shards so it would be easier and safer to gain access. All the time I took care not to leave any fingerprints although, after the day's events, I may as well have had a beacon over my head. Still! They would have to prove it!

I exited the premises within minutes of going in, with a large biscuit tin that contained the money I had seen on numerous occasions and then made my way across the nearby fields. In the blink of an eye I had the grand sum of £286, and yet I had been labouring away for 40 hours for just £6 per week, all the time enduring a prejudiced attitude from much of the workforce. I felt no remorse, and in actual fact, hoped that the majority of the money belonged to the individuals who had snubbed me so blatantly. Up yours! You wankers!

I wasn't exactly the smartest burglar in the world and it didn't take long before the local police came knocking at my grandma's door inquiring as to my whereabouts. My grandma, bless her, proclaimed my innocence and asked them to leave me alone and that I had turned over a new leaf and was, in actual fact, at work.

I could imagine her disappointment when she had been given the full facts and selfishly I had given no consideration to the fact that the shame of this particular misdeed would be magnified tenfold on account of it being my father's place of work. It would serve no purpose telling him whilst he was ill and in hospital.

Once the coast was clear I went and discussed with my grandma exactly what had taken place, and to say she was a little angry would be an understatement – it was made clear I wasn't welcome in the home any more.

I tried to give her some of my ill-gotten gains but she ushered me out with the words 'dirty money' ringing in my ears. My emotions were split because I knew that I couldn't let those people put me down any more, but I had now given them the chance to reaffirm their biased opinions towards me. I was to meet many more people similar to these over the years.

That night I found myself round a friend's house, whose mother listened carefully whilst I gave a full account of my predicament. Maybe my father would forgive me anything, except what had just taken place. My friend's mother completely surprised me by informing me that she had been close to my mother and had maintained contact all of these years. This information completely took my breath away as I had never even as much as seen a photograph of my birth mother.

I went to sleep excitedly, knowing already what I was about to do once I awoke. The decision was made more readily due to the fact that the police were in need of an interview with me, along with the difficult conversation that lay ahead with my father.

I wished my friend and his mother farewell and with an air of excitement I set off to the local train station on an adventure I never thought I would ever be able to make. I was excited. I was about to meet my mother for the very first time!

CHAPTER 6

I had always had a sense of adventure but this was something completely different, and I hadn't ventured very far in the world with regard to mileage, as I had only visited the likes of Huddersfield and Leeds, which were located within a short distance of Dewsbury.

This was a little different. The only information I had was that my mum resided in a town in the West Midlands called Nuneaton, and I did not have a clue as to how to actually find it.

This was to be the biggest adventure of my life and I was filled with trepidation, intrigue, excitement, and just about every emotion imaginable. My head was racing constantly, simply trying to comprehend the steps that I was about to take, but I had wondered for many years if this encounter would ever take place.

Had I not, on many occasions, envied the other children around me on celebratory events such as

Christmas and birthdays, and felt a sense of emptiness due to the absence of any maternal love?

Although in the early stages of my decision I had felt some form of reservation in my heart and mind, I knew this was a journey that needed to be completed.

As I purchased my ticket at the local train station with some of the proceeds of the burglary I had committed, the realisation set in that I would have to be careful that I did not arouse any suspicions to the fact that I was travelling alone, for fear that this would bring unwanted attention from the authorities. I therefore chose to attempt to map out my own timetable, although the only assured thing I knew was Nuneaton was not far from Birmingham.

The first part of the journey passed off without event, and although other passengers spoke to me, my attention was elsewhere, awash with the possibility of meeting my mother and wondering what sort of reception could I expect. As I travelled towards the Midlands I was safe in the knowledge that I would slowly but surely reach my destination. I discovered that I was to change trains at Sheffield and then once again at Derby, before finally arriving at Birmingham. I would deal with the formalities of reaching Nuneaton once I had arrived at New Street station in Birmingham.

I was not to know it at the time, but in later years I would come to realise that train stations were a familiar hunting ground for predatory paedophiles, and upon arriving at Derby Railway Station I was to discover I had a wait in excess of an hour before I could board my connecting train to Birmingham.

Whilst I waited on the platform I became aware of a male individual observing me from a distance on regular occasions. I had a lot of time to kill and so decided to walk around the station from platform to platform, but the stranger seemed to be there at every turn and my innocent mind was at a loss as to his interest in me.

I decided very quickly to place myself in the company of other passengers and hurriedly made my way back to my original platform and what I believed to be the safety of the waiting room located there. I tried to blend in with the others in the waiting room, even trying to give the impression that I was in company with them. Looking back now, it would have been patently obvious that I was travelling alone and a vulnerable target. I began to feel a little concerned for my safety and I had even more reason to be anxious when I noticed the stranger was now in the company of another man, and whilst they were in deep conversation, they would constantly look in my direction.

My train of thought, bearing in mind that I was not even aware that paedophiles existed, was that I was maybe about to be robbed of the £200 which sat comfortably in my pocket right now with my hand clasped around it. The amount of trouble this money had got me into on numerous fronts meant that I was not going to part with it easily, no matter what the circumstances were, and I considered going to the public toilets on the platform to secret the money about my person. Immediately I realised this would be a rash idea, as I would be making myself a sitting target in that setting, and so decided to stay among the safety in numbers whilst I attempted to gather my thoughts and search for a solution to this dilemma.

I would not have to wait for long as I heard a fellow passenger in the waiting room declare that the Birmingham train had just pulled in, and I hastily decamped and hurriedly made for the sanctuary the train offered. After getting on board I quickly locked myself in the toilet compartment on the train.

My head was racing and I was in a blind panic as I considered hiding the money in the toilet and retrieving it at a later stage of the journey, but I soon rejected that idea as I made the smallest of incisions in the lining of my leather jacket and inserted the ill-gotten gains and poked the money around until it sat comfortably in the small of my back. With hindsight I should have remained in the toilet compartment until the train actually pulled out but, with the comfort of knowing that the money was in what I deemed to be a safe location, I had perhaps lulled myself into a false sense of security.

Upon leaving the toilets I decided to adopt the same tactics as before and never leave myself alone under any circumstances. I came across a young woman seated in a compartment by herself, so I quickly slid the door open and sat down opposite her after exchanging smiles.

She remarked that I seemed a little flustered, and I told her a little of the recent events, but almost as soon as I had relayed this information my heart was in my mouth as I noticed my two pursuers were at the door of the carriage. Once they opened the door they claimed to be police officers and inquired as to why I was travelling alone, bombarding me with lots of questions.

Fortunately 'Janice', the lady in the carriage, was much more worldly-wise than me and demanded to see some form of official identification from the supposed 'police officers', for which none was forthcoming. After assuring them in no uncertain manner that I was no longer travelling alone and she would ensure that I reached my destination safely, the 'officers' left the train rather sheepishly.

She had introduced herself as Janice, and I was quite truthful with her as to why I believed they were about to rob me, and as the journey to Birmingham began we spoke of all sorts of things, and it transpired that 'Janice' would commute to London regularly to earn money by working in the strip clubs.

I tried to pretend I was a man of the world and understood much of what she was saying, but I was still a little naive at the time. However, I did understand by now that she had a much more significant judgement on life and the people in it than I had, and I was more than prepared to listen to her warnings of the 'bad men' who lurk in the shadows.

I would probably never get the opportunity to thank Janice personally for her actions that day, but obviously knowing what I know now I am almost certain I was saved from a sight more than a street robbery. God bless you lady! Wherever you are!

I was very taken aback by the hustle and bustle of Birmingham Station, and although I was aware that the police presence appeared to be more than sufficient it mattered little as it soon became apparent, for all my tender years, that I was simply another face in the crowd. I was about to make the last leg of my journey and I found myself a seat on a much smaller train than the ones I had previously travelled on.

I reached my destination in the middle of the afternoon and quickly realised that Nuneaton was a small town, similar to Dewsbury, the one I had just left. After approaching several people, showing them the small piece of paper with the address written on where my mother dwelt I was getting no joy. No one seemed to know of its whereabouts and I sat down, at a loss as to what to do next.

I decided to take the bull by the horns and simply went into the local police station to ask for directions. I knew I wouldn't have been reported as a runaway and, had they inquired, I would have been safe in that respect.

It transpired that a female police officer knew of my mother for whatever reason, and her place of residence. After making some initial inquiries with my mother it seemed that she was just as intrigued to meet me.

I had been placed in a cell while these formalities had taken place and my cell door was opened, and I was informed I was about to be given transport to Cross Street in Stockingford, a suburb of Nuneaton. I was glad to see the back of the cell, before any of my misdemeanours surfaced during their inquiries, but I would see a Nuneaton cell many more times in the coming years. So I was finally to meet my mother and it wasn't quite the entrance I would have preferred, being in the back of a police car, but here I was!

No one who has not been in this situation could even begin to explain this scenario. I stared at my mother open-mouthed in amazement at how beautiful she was. I looked at her face for so long, seeing a lot of my own features in her, and I was dumbstruck at the close resemblance that I failed to notice she was in the latter stages of pregnancy with who I now know to be my brother, Glenn.

We gorged on the information we relayed to each other. I was made aware that I had an extended family consisting of three brothers, Patrick, Stephen, and James, plus three sisters, Tania, Susan, and Dawn and Glenn on the way, to be followed by Craig the following year.

My mother's partner's name, Glenn's father, was Dan Darby, and in later years I learnt to love this man as my father for the goodness he showed me, but I would resent him for many years for events that are about to unfold.

After the initial question and answers session my mother and I had just participated in, an uneasy silence followed. No situation is stranger than the one we both found ourselves in because we were mother and son, and yet comparative strangers at the same time. I discovered my siblings had been in a children's home in Sheffield and my mother had only recently managed to get them back into her custody due to Dan's involvement in her life, and I have nothing but admiration for the man and his assistance in doing this. The problem now was that I was much older than the other children and I was not going to be the best example for them to look up to. Hadn't I already made my debut in the back of a police car?

I perhaps knew my days were numbered, but not as quickly as it actually came about. I had enjoyed the experience of spending time with my younger brothers and sisters and at every opportunity took them down to the nearby town centre, spoiling them as often as possible.

Questions were beginning to be asked as to how I could afford these jaunts, and it soon came to light as to why I had actually run away in the first place. I had barely settled into what seemed a perfect family life to me when the carpet was pulled from beneath my feet. It was no more than I could have expected really on reflection but, none the less, I was about to feel an emptiness and rejection which I could never have envisaged when I began this incredible journey. It had been intimated on more than one occasion that I should consider going back to Yorkshire, but selfishly I had chosen to ignore the hints.

On most days after the children had gone to school I would sit with my mother, and we would help each other to fill in the gaps whilst Dan was at work. Unusually on this particular day my mother had not returned from the school run and so I wiled away the morning by myself. When Dan came home on his lunch break from work he seemed surprised that I was still there, and it became clear that my mother had been given the unenviable task of telling me I had to go. At least I had the consolation of leaving with the knowledge that my mother's loyalty to me made it an impossible task.

Dan was quite a blunt man, and he made it quite clear that he did not want to end his shift later that evening with me still in attendance, so he had decided to give me a lift to the train station now, as this matter needed bringing to a conclusion. I very much resented all of this at the time but, in years to come, I would readily be able to understand his reasoning. He was responsible for the safety and well-being of six minors and I was to be 'top-of-the-tree' as far as bad influences were concerned.

Not a lot was said as we made the short journey, and I was maybe thinking I may get a last minute reprieve and he would throw his arms around me, but Dan was a realist and already had his work cut out rearing the other children – I was more than likely to be a problem child that he didn't need. I was to be someone else's problem once again and it would be many more years before I had the urge or the courage to visit Nuneaton again.

I was still unsure as to which route I even had to take and I asked Dan. His response was to just get on any train. North, south or whatever. In short… bye bye!

I had maybe had an hour to gather my thoughts and acclimatise myself to the fact that I was once again alone, and in a haze I sat and bit my lip. I refused to cry but I knew in my heart I could not return to Yorkshire as I felt I had betrayed my father, not only with the burglary of his works but also by coming to meet my mother.

I made the decision to do what countless other runaways had done before me and make for the bright lights of London with the streets 'paved with gold'! Hadn't Janice told me funny accounts of life in London? I hoped against hope I could chance upon her when I jumped onto the train but I knew it was not to be. I would shortly find out that London's streets were certainly not paved in gold!

CHAPTER 7

If I thought Birmingham was a busy terminal then Euston train station in London was absolutely manic in comparison.

Financially I was still a little secure and I would not have to go without food for the time being but here I was, a long way from home, and I felt my life had been turned completely on its head.

I had never felt sadness this deep, nor would I again, I imagined, but I had to get myself together because I had already had the scare at Derby station and my sixth sense told me London was going to be a very challenging place, alone and unloved as it appeared.

I had a little roam about the local area by the train station, wary of venturing too far and seemingly ending up back by the terminal almost as soon as I'd left. I may as well have been one of the many pigeons that frequented the place, I returned that often. On one of my jaunts I managed to purchase a small pocket knife with my safety in mind, although this incident resulted in me carrying and using knives for many years to come.

Day turned into night quite quickly, and I began to get cold, and although passengers were permitted to remain in the confines of the station if they were able to produce a current travel ticket, I preferred not to, thereby not coming to the attention of the local constabulary or any other misfortune that may befall me. As I scavenged about around the station I managed to discover a disused old mailbag, and although it was in a dirty state I placed my legs in it and pulled it about me as best I possibly could, welcoming the meagre warmth that the canvas material offered. My first night in London was to be far from memorable and I certainly didn't feel that the bright lights had given me the best welcome.

My mind was troubled as I attempted to find the solace of sleep. But finally, sleep I did, and once I realised that morning had broken I felt a little safer knowing I had survived whatever fears had been causing me concern. I presumed I would need the limited comfort that my makeshift sleeping bag had offered me again so I concealed it as best I could until the next time I might need it.

I spent long hours during the day watching train after train arrive from Birmingham, for some strange reason, perhaps subconsciously feeling 'Janice' would alight from one of them. It would never happen and I knew this more as each day passed.

I was searching and in need of any sort of compassion. I had never felt this alone before and I became fearful of talking to anyone for fear that they had ulterior motives. After the incident in Derby I had become more cautious and paranoid.

Days stretched into weeks, and I returned each night to

my makeshift camp. I would cleanse myself during the day at the local 'wash-and-brush-up' facilities as best I could, but eventually my clothes began to be a little worse for wear and eventually I bought some new jeans and a very heavy woollen jumper, not with fashion in mind, but to give me added warmth on the colder evenings.

I would see other people in the wash and brush up who appeared to be in the same situation as myself but I didn't have any inclination to converse with any of them, bearing in mind I still had ample financial assets to feed me for a good while longer yet.

I would speak throughout the day to various people who appeared to be tourist types, and therefore safer to approach. I hadn't intended to set about begging and didn't think I would be even capable of such an exercise but, one day, and without any prompting by myself, a complete stranger squeezed a few shillings into my hand. Not that I'd noticed but I had gained an unkempt, bedraggled appearance, and without me even uttering a word someone had come to the conclusion I was looking for alms for the poor! I didn't have time to be embarrassed and readily accepted any monies proffered, and in no time whatsoever even found myself comfortably asking any stranger at all for money. I soon became adept at opening my eyes in a doleful manner, gaining as much sympathy and generosity as was forthcoming. I envisaged myself as being of a similar nature to earlier Dickensian urchins as on certain days I would most certainly not have been a sight to behold.

I was surviving comfortably and even dared venture out and about and actually take in a lot more of central London, albeit always like a homing pigeon, returning to Euston station where I felt secure. I had stopped dwelling on my misfortune because the reality was I was now in a situation where I was just becoming accustomed, by instinct, to simply deal with my circumstances, and it just developed into, strangely enough, an everyday 'normal' lifestyle or at least my way of life. I was becoming very thick-skinned and nothing whatsoever phased me anymore, which should have surprised me but didn't.

When I first arrived in London I was like a rabbit caught in headlights and a very timid individual but, overnight, I had become an established figure in certain circles. It wouldn't be a path I would recommend to everyone but I had found my feet in life much quicker, and I had a streetwise confidence and swagger about me which I would never have thought possible four weeks earlier. I was known to lots of people by now although I had never confided in anyone as to where I actually slept each night.

By now I was a reasonably good judge of character and by chance I met some very strange but amiable people who were much older than me but gave me a sense of belonging, even if it was for a short while, and the following day I was pleased when they were still in the same area.

On one occasion, as the group prepared to depart from my patch, I simply ambled along with them and as they didn't seem to object I soon found myself in an area I now know to be Holloway. After hurdling and scaling a few minor obstacles I found myself in what seemed to be a communal home belonging to them.

In actual fact it was no more than a squat where maybe thirty people resided and looked after each other's interests and needs. Knowing what I do now these people at the time would have been called subversives or extremists, when in actual fact they were no more than a band of comrades who pooled their resources and cared for each other.

Who was I to complain? I had gone from a hessian mailbag by some walkway to almost having my own room with several blankets, and at this rate of progress surely I would soon have an apartment in Knightsbridge or

Mayfair! Things were looking up and the camaraderie that existed amongst these people could not be matched. I had a serious feeling of belonging amongst these 'crusties', 'hippies', or whatever public opinion cared to call them. I was to learn to have a view on most things and each subject, I listened to the level of understanding and awareness, they had soon convinced me that they were educated people.

I was soon to be introduced to a joint of marijuana while we sat around the fire, quickly followed by a trip of LSD which took my mind to places I never ever thought possible. My first trip, fortunately, proved to be a pleasant one and in the years to come I would take many more. But for the time being this first time could never be recaptured again. Everything was so vivid and colourful and I would never experience such euphoria at this level again. I was unprepared for what might happen and I simply revelled in that night and could never, nor would I want to, forget that night, ever.

I felt as safe as I had ever done since arriving in London and not one person would dictate to me or try to correct my behaviour. I was a free spirit and would be encouraged to do whatever I liked, within reason.

This was my adopted family and although I thought back to my home in Yorkshire very little, I knew that eventually I would have to perhaps give them the comfort of knowing that no harm had come to me and, if anything, I regarded myself as being in a very safe environment. But I was having so much fun that I just never seemed to get around to contacting home and time went by in lots of drug-induced states and I felt as if I didn't have a past, and this was what I'd always known and nothing before mattered.

We went to other squats on most evenings and I would watch intently as the others became embroiled in very loud political debate but only till the spliffs began to circulate and lessen the conversation until the preference was for music, and in the blink of an eye a full party would be in progress. I would love these occasions because not only was I becoming politically aware, but I also had a good social life and free drugs seemed to be in constant supply.

I had also been introduced to the heady world of festivals and live music and we travelled around from venue to venue in a battered old bus which would get us to our destination. On the rare occasion that the bus was not to be found due to one of the other 'residents' being in possession of it, we would quite simply take to the road and hitchhike in pairs. This gave me the opportunity to appreciate our complex motorway systems.

I often noticed the big sign indicating 'THE NORTH' and had a good command of my bearings – at a future time I would need to know this information. I did dwell on my 'previous life' from time to time, albeit with more consideration for my grandmother rather than my father or my fleeting introduction to my mother.

Shortly after returning from one of our outings to an alternative squatters' camp, after having a good night's entertainment, all hell broke loose as the local police must have decided enough was enough and very heavy-handedly not only raided our premises, but practically demolished them. My lasting memory, as I clambered out of the rear window, was, why was there any need to bring about so much mayhem? Especially considering most of the inhabitants of the squat were very peacefully minded people. Maybe the drug situation had spiralled out of control, or maybe the police were simply bored on that particular evening and decided to have a little fun at our expense. I made myself scarce, mindful of the fact that I may receive some awkward questioning about my age and identity. Time had passed by and I would perhaps be causing concern with my continued absence in Yorkshire and I was not prepared to give up on my adventure this easily.

I imagined we would all regroup at some later stage at the squat, but it was not to be, and search though I may, our band of brothers seemed to have been disbanded. No way could I have ever returned to my original sleeping arrangements outside Euston station and so, with a heavy heart, I reluctantly decided to put into practice the method I had been taught, and I raised my thumb in the air and headed for the sign for the M1 and 'THE NORTH'. I had no qualms about doing this as I had done it on other occasions, but it did not take me too long to realise why it was safer to do so in pairs!

My first lift was a middle-aged delivery driver in a small van, and he perhaps relished a little company to kill the hours and the miles on the motorway and I was more than a good conversationalist whilst I gave him accounts of my recent soirées. Obviously leaving certain parts out. He dropped me close to Leicester Forest Services and wished me well for the remainder of the journey. He had been quite amiable, but with my next lift I was not to be so fortunate.

I had read signs, whilst I waited, indicating Nuneaton, but my memory of that place was a hard one to swallow and for many years I would hate even hearing the name of the town! A large truck pulled over and the driver asked me where I was headed and I told him Leeds! He replied that he could take me as far as Nottingham and I readily jumped in, having already stood at the same junction for several hours and feeling rather cold. I had barely begun to get settled and engage in conversation with the driver when the earlier friendly topics began to take on a more sinister tone. Some of the remarks took on more of a sexual nature and I was asked how many times I had 'done it' and which girls I preferred. I felt very uncomfortable with the continual line of questioning and tried to change the subject on several occasions, but it fell on deaf ears.

Suddenly and without warning he placed his hand on

my knee, informing me that if I chose to be really nice to him he could perhaps drive me all the way to my intended destination, Leeds. I reached down to my sock and pulled out my small knife and pushed it towards the driver's neck, insisting that I wished to travel no further and that he should pull over immediately. Although I was a little afraid I would be prepared to use it if necessary and I'm certain the man realised this, because rather than continue to what would have been a perfectly legal drop-off junction, he pulled onto the hard shoulder at the first opportunity. I got out, shaken but unharmed, and promised myself to assess my next proposed lift a little more carefully than I had the last one.

After gathering my composure I proceeded on my way and reached my destination without any further incident. I had taken the last leg of my journey on a local bus as I still had a few coppers in my pocket and I smiled a little as I recognised familiar landmarks. It wasn't exactly home-sweet-home but for the foreseeable future it was all I had. Little did I know that events were about to take a serious turn for the worst and the news I was about to hear would leave me speechless.

I made my way up the stairs to my family home and, to my surprise, the door was locked, and after knocking several times with no response, I stood there at a loss as to what to do. Some of the smaller children from the estate began to stare and one of the tiniest of them said to me, quite casually, "Your father's dead." He was not to know the magnitude of what he had just told me, being as how he was very young and had said it as off-handedly as you would maybe give someone the outcome of a football match. I was overcome with every emotion imaginable. Guilt, remorse, selfishness, and a very large helping of emptiness and loss.

After enquiring at close-by addresses as to the whereabouts of my grandmother and discovering that she was at my dad's brother's abode, staying with the family. I made my way there, not knowing what reception to expect, but almost certainly not a cordial one.

My grandmother squeezed me so tightly I thought I would burst, but I wasn't the most welcome visitor at this particular time, and my intuition made me leave almost as soon as I had arrived. I made my excuses and left, feeling that I was adding to my grandmother's sorrow. I promised to return at the earliest opportunity, but the police would put paid to that idea, because within the next few days I would find myself in that all too familiar place that seemed to blight my life. In the back of a police car!

CHAPTER 8

I was to be charged with burglary of my previous place of employment and would be held in custody until my court appearance at Dewsbury Magistrates. I was, once again, placed in the cells below the Town Hall – my all too familiar habitat. Over the coming years it would be a toss-up as to whether I spent more time inside these cells or inside my wellies as a youth.

Anyone who has been incarcerated in this ancient cell block will readily concur that sleep comes with difficulty due to the Town Hall clock above chiming and reverberating every fifteen minutes, culminating in an increased decibel on the hour. Our very own version of 'Big Ben' right on our doorstep!

It was beneficial to be half awake, as it happens, because these were the times when impromptu interviews would often take place in the cells. No friendly greetings or solicitors present at interviews here.

Times had moved on from a good old-fashioned clip round the ear from the friendly local neighbourhood bobby. I loathed being detained in this cell block because Dewsbury police at that time had more than their share of bullies within their ranks.

I was 'encouraged' to admit to having committed many a crime that I didn't have a clue about. I would be told I was about to be sent down anyway so it would be irrelevant how many charges I actually faced. I was intimidated time after time into looking again at certain offences that they would want to be cleared up and taken into consideration. The officers attempted to wind up the outstanding crimes which would, in turn, gain them a 'pat on the back' from their governor by lowering the crime statistics.

I imagine it would give them the easy life when they were on duty because there would be no need to carry out prolonged investigations if they could simply physically assault whoever it was that happened to be in the cells until they admitted crimes that they had not done.

Modern day cell blocks are monitored vigilantly nowadays, but for anyone to doubt that in days gone by the police did not resort to the tactics I have just described, you are walking about with blinkers on!

On one occasion, a particularly sadistic detective sergeant 'suggested' to me over and over that I was responsible for a certain burglary, and circled me like some predatory shark. Whilst he did so he sharpened a pencil. He would make sure I watched his every move while he and his colleague laughed at my reluctance to 'confess'. He walked around without doing anything, but once or twice when I wasn't prepared he would stick the sharpened pencil into my neck, and as you can imagine, it would cause me great pain. I never knew when the next jab would come from so I would attempt to swivel my head to see exactly where he was but his colleague would kick me on my ankle, thereby distracting my attention, and I had a double-pronged attack to defend.

Dewsbury police were notorious for browbeating prisoners and I defy anyone to claim that in that set of circumstances they would not confess to crimes they had not committed. I was a young child for Christ's sake, and the brutality has remained with me throughout my life.

I hear also the views of people claiming that we prisoners deserve a fate befitting the crime, and had we not placed ourselves in this predicament in the first place then we would not have encountered the 'treatment' that we did. I would like to state here and now that I never at any time, throughout all of my criminality, burgled anyone's home and would prefer office burglaries. I do not state this to lessen my crimes, nor do I condone my behaviour, but I would find myself in a set of circumstances beyond my control.

I would imagine that my torturers of the day had long and lengthy police careers with countless commendations and promotions. The hypocrisy within all of you disgusts me and I most certainly will never raise a glass to support men of standing. Pillars of society!

Don't make me laugh!

I would admit to several offences that were nothing whatsoever to do with me and await my punishment. It was decided that I would be sent to a Catholic Approved School by the name of Saint Camillus in Sherbourne-in-Elmet, close to Tadcaster in Yorkshire.

I had my reservations, but if I thought this place would have the same rigorous regime as the previous detention centre I would be mistaken. My description of it would be to say it was run along the lines of a preparatory boarding school, albeit without the fees, and it consisted of three large dormitory blocks that I shall call blocks A, B and C. If boys behaved during term times they would be allowed to go home during school holidays, exactly the same as you would be permitted at a regular everyday establishment in the 'free world'.

On the occasions when the majority of the boys would be allowed home, the 'school' would resemble a ghost town, consisting of some individuals who had misbehaved and the residue, the group which I belonged to, who had no homes to actually go to.

My grandmother now resided with other family members and I had no home as such and no one wanted the responsibility of a juvenile who had gone off the rails to the extent that I had. So, not for the first time, I found myself alone in the world and unwanted.

For a short while I was allocated a place in the bricklaying group, and on reflection, I should have set about learning a trade, but I took exception to being used as cheap physical labour and I recalled the easier option of education, which was readily available, and yet again found myself in the classroom.

A lot of the other boys preferred to learn the trades available such as welding, carpentry, plastering, or bricklaying. So in the classroom the personal tuition was of a kind I had never known, and I gathered information as a sponge would gather water.

For the first time in my life I actually enjoyed being in receipt of further education and I would go about my work diligently. I would settle into everyday life at the Approved School readily and bond with lots of boys, and discover I wasn't the only one who had been dealt a bad hand in life.

It wasn't long, however, before I began to resent the other boys going home to at least have some sort of respite from their situation. I felt that I too deserved a little respite. I absconded on at least six occasions, and each time I was caught I would be duly returned to the Approved School to receive a severe caning, and that would be the end of the matter. All things considered, the rewards of those decamps were well worth the discomfort of what turned out to be corporal punishment across the buttocks at the school. Sometimes I would run away alone and other times in groups, and as long as any crimes committed whilst on the run did not warrant serious charges or further court appearances, we would always be accepted back into the fold. Not exactly with open arms, but we cared little.

I would subsequently be wise enough to know how to avoid any road or highway after my first excursion with my thumb out had brought me to the attention of the police within about half an hour of me scaling the wall. Each time after that I would make for the railway lines and follow the tracks for mile after mile. The added bonus was that eventually I would come across secluded train stations and be given the opportunity to burgle the premises and acquire some ready cash, and also some train tickets to be used at a later stage.

Sometimes I would be caught within days and other times it would be weeks. I wasn't exactly inconspicuous considering I would have to beg, borrow and steal throughout my absences. During the times when I would decamp with other boys I had become friendly with, we would, in turn, visit each other's places of birth such as Newcastle, Stockport, Rotherham, or anywhere that took our fancy.

There was one occasion when three of us, on the spur of the moment, decided that once the night watchman had completed one of his rounds during the night we would be gone within minutes, thereby giving ourselves perhaps a two-hour start. I had remembered from my brief time in the bricklaying department where the instructor left the key to the dumper truck. Two of us would sit in the bucket while Paul, who was a proficient driver, would do the steering job. I don't think any of us had laughed as much in our whole lives as we did now, meandering down the country lanes. This was taking the adventures of Tom Sawyer to a completely different level, and how we never crashed is beyond me. God only knows what health and safety guidelines we failed to adhere to that night!

Somehow, by chance and good fortune rather than our expertise, we arrived at Tadcaster and left the truck by the side of the road and hid by the train station until the early morning trains would be available for us to jump on, hopefully going to whichever location we had planned for.

These adventures would be the highlight of our stay at the Approved School and filled us with much humour for many weeks after our recapture. The other boys would be afforded the reward of regular home visits, so why should we be criticised for arranging our own little breaks from the monotony? We were waifs and strays who no one wanted, but we were also young boys deserving of some fun.

The home was run by masters rather than wardens and the principal of the school was a retired army major who resided in the big house within the grounds so that he could be accessed easily if there should be any serious incident.

On most weekends we could hear the sounds of revelry from the major's house as it transpired that he would have parties regularly for the staff. We quickly gathered that the alcohol would be in the major's adjacent garage and foolishly thought that if we should purloin a little of it, we could maybe have our own party and it would go unnoticed. We were to learn otherwise when the matter came to light due to our own drunken rowdiness, and some of the other boys didn't hesitate to point the finger at the usual three suspects.

When we had been given the cane across our buttocks on previous occasions it would in no way resemble the beating I was about to endure. My arms were held firmly just below the elbow from the opposite side of the conference table in the main hall, and my trousers were pulled down to my ankles, and in front of everyone assembled, I was thrashed until my buttocks bled and the cane would wrap around my legs, causing deep welts on my outer thighs. We had committed the cardinal sin and overstepped the mark with the theft of the major's alcohol, and he was maybe setting an example to the others in attendance that there must never be a recurrence of what had just taken place.

The discomfort in my lower body over the following weeks ensured that I would never go within 100 yards of the garage again, but eventually we would all learn to laugh and smile again, recollecting the enormity of what we had done. It was a victory of sorts and a sore bum would be worth the triumph.

I would never get the opportunity to go anywhere and I think the school began to appreciate that fact, and started to create other opportunities for me. I had started to get involved in the Duke of Edinburgh Awards Scheme for young people which meant I had to complete unending tasks such as map reading on the Yorkshire Moors and learning how to survive camping out in very adverse conditions. I had decided to achieve the bronze and silver awards but had reservations about competing for the gold one, as I knew this meant coming into contact with the duke and I had no inclination to meet anyone with royal status as I had developed an aversion to what they represented.

One of my tasks entailed having to make my own way from the local railway station at Church Fenton to Chigwell in Essex to a holiday camp for the disabled. I would find this task quite easy being as how I'd practically lived on the railway lines in the preceding months and, if anything, I was an expert in rail travel!

On arrival at the holiday camp I was informed that I

would be in charge and solely responsible for a room with four occupants. Two of which could do everyday tasks themselves but the other two would need me to bath, shave, feed and take care of any toilet needs. One of my occupants was a man I shall call Bill, whose legs had been riddled with machine gun fire in an earlier war, and I would learn to feel humble in the presence of this man.

The Approved School authorities had given me the chance to leave the school premises with the trust that I would complete my duties and even return as and when instructed. I discovered a lot about myself in that month-long period and had no qualms about wiping a man's posterior after he had completed his toilet duties, or even the same with his bed sheets when he had the occasional accident. How could I even begin to complain? Bill was an unheralded hero in my eyes.

I returned to the Approved School with a rewarding feeling of euphoria about me. Caring for Bill and the others, with their different disabilities and the obstacles they overcame each day, opened my eyes to the realities of the world. The experience humbled me more than anything before or since. It wasn't long however before I returned to my old ways, and decided once again to abscond, but this time I would not be returning.

In the office in each dormitory everyone's cigarettes would be kept in a secure drawer with whichever individual's name upon the packet, and they would be permitted one cigarette out of the packet after each meal. Before absconding I had broken into the office and stolen all of the cigarettes, thereby ensuring my journey would not be lacking by way of nicotine. I had not, selfishly, given any consideration to the ill-feeling this would create when the others had awoke, ate their breakfast, and then discovered they had no cigarettes.

Getting to Morley train station, close to Leeds, I had, as before, burgled the ticket office but was discovered and held until the police arrived. The police were informed that they should charge me as I would not be welcome back at the school. In hindsight it was perhaps a wise decision because my safety could not be assured at the school, because the other boys would want to give me more than a few choice words!

My wake-up call was about to arrive. I would be going to Big School! I was now on the roll call of the very secure confines of Thope Arch Remand Centre in Wetherby whilst I once again awaited my fate. I would now be in the sort of setting which would become my way of life for many years to come.

CHAPTER 9

The first smell that greeted me upon entering my cell was the stench of stale urine coming from the chamber pot in the corner, the contents of which the previous occupant had so kindly overlooked emptying. This visit was to be no cup of tea. Some cells had two inmates, and some consisted of three in times of overcrowding. We would be locked up for all but one hour of the day permitted for exercise, but, should it rain, we would forfeit the exercise period for that day and, needless to say, those days would be long and very boring.

I would witness on the block facing mine, the inmates swinging their plastic tea mugs, with cotton unravelled from blankets, from cell to cell and even from landing to landing quite expertly. Stopping only to gather the contraband in quickly should a warder appear doing his rounds with his dog. I soon longed for the comfort of my room at the approved school, but I would need to dispense with these thoughts. I had made my bed and would need to lie on it and come to terms with my circumstances. Whilst I had been in the approved school I had been placed on a waiting list at St. James' Hospital in Leeds for tattoo removal of the cross that still remained prominently on my chin. I should have been top of the list but I took second place to a boy from Sunderland who had a third eye tattooed in the middle of his forehead, giving me comfort that I wasn't the only juvenile to do something a little strange. But my turn came around and I was informed by the governor I would be transported to the hospital, but with added security because of my tendency to abscond. The hospital in later years would become famous for all the wrong reasons after being renamed 'Jimmys' because of the Disc Jockey Jimmy Saville's patronage.

I was taken to the hospital under escort and handcuffed at all times until such time as I was given a local anaesthetic and sedated a little. Lots of progress has been made since those days regarding removal techniques, but in those days it was a basic procedure of cutting out the offending item and pulling the skin together tightly and stitching the area up again. Obviously it worked to a certain degree, although to this day I am still left with the remnants of the tattoo, and people often ask me what the blue mark on my chin is. Being from the North of England where the mining industry once flourished I would often just declare that the remaining blue mark of the cross was from a mining injury which had gathered some coal dust and left a mining scar.

I returned to the remand centre in a great deal of pain and my chin twice the size it had been before, and once the numbness had wore off, it became patently obvious that the stitches had been put in far too tightly. The first meal I had since completion of the operation was accepted gladly, but as I opened my mouth to take in the first food of the day I must have opened a fraction too far, and some of the stitches popped and once again opened up the wound. I was bleeding profusely as I rang the panic bell situated by the door and was immediately rushed to the medical area and patched up to stem the blood flow. On my next visit to the hospital they denied that they were responsible for any negligence, and despite my many complaints they insisted they had followed procedures to the letter. It soon became clear to me that the tattoo removal operation had been a failure and I was to be left with a permanent reminder.

I would have a succession of different cell mates over a period of time. Some would have applied for bail through their solicitors and obtained it. There was no such consideration for me as I was regarded as having a high risk of failing to attend any hearing. I would never apply anyway because I did not have anyone to vouch for me, and the main condition of any bail consideration is to have a safe house of residence, therefore it would be futile for me to even consider any application. Instead I would be expected to remain in the remand centre and await the grand opening of the quarter sessions in Leeds, which would later be renamed Leeds Assizes and finally a Crown Court many years later.

I was told by some of the other inmates that, on the opening day of these quarter sessions, the opening ceremony would be heralded by numerous men in multi-coloured costumes, blowing on trumpets. I had no reason to disbelieve this. Our country always has had a morbid fascination with pomp and pageantry.

Should any of us miss the three-monthly sitting and not be on the list, we would be placed on the next sessions list, but have to spend another season on remand. This peeved many a prisoner because, at that time, any period spent on remand did not come off your actual sentence, so in effect you would be serving two different sentences. The only benefit of being on remand was because you remained unconvicted and it was possible to be visited daily and have certain luxuries brought in. Not that this applied to me. I wouldn't even receive mail, let alone any visits or luxuries!

One day I was lolling about in the exercise yard taking in the warm sunshine we were experiencing that day, when we noticed one of the warders heading in our direction. We quickly passed the joint we had been smoking along the line, thinking the sweet aroma had reached his attention and we were about to be frog-marched back to our cells.

Never has a joint been passed around so quickly. We need not have worried as I was the sole purpose of his interest, and I was requested to follow him to the principal's office, which was on my landing.

There was a 'cat-and-mouse' bout of questioning while the principal tried to glean from me just how close I was to my grandma before informing me that, after a bout of ill health, she had died.

These formalities in a prison are done to try to determine whether you should be allowed to attend funerals. In most cases it must be a close relative such as immediate parents or any request is refused. Especially if you are regarded as a potential escapee.

He was satisfied enough with my explanations that my grandma had been my mainstay in life and therefore I was given permission, once again, to attend under escort.

I had never even once been notified that my grandmother had been ill, let alone had had a relapse. I was out of sight and out of mind to a lot of people, and I was filled with anger. I would have to bite my lip for fear that my attendance at her funeral would be withdrawn.

So it was with that I found myself at the church of my youth, Saint Paulinus in all of its splendour and, although the warders draped a coat over my handcuffs to give the impression I wasn't manacled, a lot of the congregation would be aware that I was a detainee and it always amazed me that, in perhaps the one and only place where you should show your 'Christian' attitude, these pious individuals preferred to shun me like the proverbial leper. I was greeted warmly by a few and I knew in my heart before I arrived the people it would be. I would feel the tears running down my face and the warders would prefer not to notice, being embarrassed themselves to be in the company of strangers at such a sad time.

I went back to the Remand Centre with a very heavy heart. I was now completely alone. Both my figureheads in life had died in quite a short timescale, and this time for sure I had nothing and no one, and whilst I had now graduated to 'Big School', the future was bleak. I did not wish to even leave the confines of my cell, and even fellow cellmates had requested to be located to an alternative cell because of my mood swings, which would be too much for them to comprehend. Little did I know but these bouts of depression would dog me for the rest of my life and I would require continued psychiatric assessment and care.

I had not been out on to the exercise yards for days and was becoming reclusive, and when one officer was insistent that I must go out whether I liked it or not and pushed me onto the landing and closed my cell door behind me, I was infuriated. I found myself out on the yard but without any company as my black mood would depress the others and they preferred giving me a very wide berth. I was determined it would not happen the following day, and with the sparse furniture I had I set about barricading myself in to the cell.

My mind was disturbed at this time and I think a lot of the warders tried to reason with me while they stood on the grass three floors below my cell location. I was in a blind rage and picked up the chamber pot from the corner of my cell and rather foolishly threw the contents out of the window and over the officers below, not realising that I had overstepped the mark this time and would get the biggest beating I would have to endure in my whole life.

The warders had contingency plans for this exact situation, and soon set about applying pressure to the cell door and literally jacking the door off its handles until they could get a hand-hold on me and pull me out into the landing.

In situations such as this all the other inmates are secured behind their doors and no one is there to witness what is about to take place, which is violence you wouldn't even dare to think was imaginable.

I was dragged by the feet along the landing to the winding staircase that led to the bottom landing and the exclusion cells, which was the solitary confinement area. At every turn there were maybe six warders making some form of physical contact, be it punches, kicks, or whatever blow is taking place and you just wait and welcome the final blow that will render you unconscious. As my feet were pulled along and down the stairwell, my head bounced off each step in turn, and the blackout I awaited would soon be forthcoming.

God knows what time I began to come around again. All I could say was I became aware that I was in plenty of pain, especially in my ribcage area, and my head seemed to be covered in blood and would require stitching. I would later learn that I had two fractured ribs and was in need of stitching for two separate wounds.

If anyone amongst you has ever had to deal with the discomfort of broken ribs you will realise the pain is immeasurable. Even the task of coughing or turning around in your bed becomes increasingly difficult and I could not even begin to describe the pain. This was life in a 1970s-themed penal institution and would be no different than any other similar establishment of the time. In our present day prisons an inmate's every move is monitored by CCTV, but no so in this era. I could complain from the highest mountain of the brutality but it would simply fall on deaf ears.

The explanation given for my injuries was that I had struggled to such an extent that I had broken free from my warders, lost my footing, and fallen down the stairs. Quite a feasible explanation in the circumstances, and I wouldn't be the first or the last convict to be presented with this cock-and-bull story, but any visiting magistrates in the day who you registered any complaint with would be so gullible you would be better saving your time and breath. It would be futile to attempt to take on the powers that be which represented the regime. It would be tantamount to running up against a brick wall. A complete and utter no-win situation!

I remained in solitary for the next few weeks. I suppose it would have served no purpose letting the other inmates see the extent of my injuries, although I would have thought it would have served as an adequate warning to them that this would be the outcome of any future misbehaviour.

It would be a long time before my ribs knitted together once again in what I would call a normal manner, but the beating had served its purpose and my earlier aggression had quickly been replaced by a sheepishness – not usually a description associated with me.

I would soon appear at my intended court and would be dealt with at the early stages of the quarter sessions, being as how my plea would be one of GUILTY! The guilty cases were dealt with early and gotten out of the way, thereby freeing up court time for the later trials and pleads of not guilty.

I was in and out as if passing through a hotel door. I

was dealt with so quickly and I received my first term of borstal training. Whatever that would turn out to be it could be no worse than what I had been through already, or so I thought!

If I thought I had been in the 'Big House' already then I had not allowed for the introduction to Armley Prison in Leeds, which was so overcrowded that it slept three to a cell and people who were due for discharge or trustees actually slept on the floor of the chapel. I kid you not! This was the reality of our prisons in the early 70s and the overcrowding was at its height.

Due to the policy of shared bedding that was quickly handed from departing inmate to arriving inmate, I managed to contract not only impetigo but also scabies, to compliment my sorry state. Although this was a mainstream adult dispersal jail a landing would be set aside for us young borstal boys, and we would be packed off to Strangeways Prison in Manchester within no time, to be assessed and dispatched to whichever borstal suited our needs. Some of us must have looked quite cute in our tender years, and we would get wolf whistled often as we exercised in the yard. I would see this as friendly banter and believe it to be a form of leg-pulling but, having said that, I would have been amongst the last to step forward to spend an evening in a shared cell with any of these admirers. I would return to Armley Jail on several occasions in the coming years, but for now I was headed for Strangeways. This prison had a more fearsome reputation than any other jail the length and breadth of the country, but I was about to pass through the gates and be amongst the youngest in there. The vastness of the prison was very much an eye-opener and consisted of wing after wing housing borstal boys sent from other city jails such as Walton in Liverpool and Durham in the North East. We would all be under the same roof in our grey trousers and navy blue tunics. We were going to be taught some discipline long before we were to be allocated to any borstal centre.

Bullying was rife and it soon became clear that it would be necessary to carry some sort of weapon to defend oneself.

I sculpted a makeshift handle from a toothbrush until I had a suitable crevice to slide a broken razor blade down, and then set about melting the blade into the handle until it was firmly set. I would take me numerous lighted matches to complete this task, but I would finally be happy with my weapon of choice. I was now in a very violent and hostile atmosphere and would need eyes everywhere. There would be reports of stabbings and slashings on a daily basis and I would constantly need to be alert.

After numerous tests over a period of time I discovered that my hall of residence would be Everthorpe Borstal Centre in Brough in the East Riding of Yorkshire. I believe I was sent to this Yorkshire centre with regard to simplifying any visits from relatives. Had they taken time to study further they would surely have noticed that I got neither mail nor visits. I had been left in this world on a 'wing-and-a-prayer' for sure. Everthorpe would be a very brutal place!

CHAPTER 10

Everthorpe consisted of four very large cell blocks and by now I readily recognised the accentual tones of Scouse, Mancunian, and the inmates of the North East. This borstal and any other would be packed to the rafters with bad boys from all these areas, and although I became friends with several of them down the years, I would need to be very wary of the majority of them. I imagined myself as a bit of a 'Jack-the-lad' but in all honesty I couldn't hold a candle to some of these characters. They were city boys and from a criminal point of view they had done and seen far more than me, although there would also be lots of 'chancers' who overrated themselves. There would be a pack-culture atmosphere amongst the city boys, and exactly as it had been on the outside, it would rear its ugly head inside here quite often. These boys would be very territorial and took offence at the slightest things, and locked horns with other rival groups at the drop of a hat. The warders would try to stifle any of the unrest that would come to their attention but they would be fighting a constantly losing battle. I would hear on a daily basis of a vicious stabbing or slashing that had taken place.

Caging 500 young men overflowing with testosterone under the same roof would always be a recipe for disaster. I had managed to avoid any violence during my first few months but all that would change when I got involved in an altercation that was none of my business.

Two inmates standing by the snooker table were involved in a very heated debate with each other and I knew one of them vaguely as I had worked with him in the borstal's kitchen area. I was in the wrong place at the wrong time and as I tried to placate the boy I knew and attempt to bring the dispute to an amicable solution, I was grabbed by the hair at the nape of my neck and whilst my head was held down on the snooker table I was continuously assaulted until I blacked out.

I was left lying on the floor for one of the warders to discover me, when any of them finally did do their duties of walking their rounds, as opposed to just sitting around in their office gossiping or reading newspapers. It was the law of the jungle in here and violence was never too far away, but the warders views seemed to be just to sit out of the way in the safe confines of their office and simply leave the lunatics to take over the asylum!

I had thought I had been punched but I later discovered that I had been dealt several blows with a snooker ball by my assailant. I had lost several teeth and required emergency dental treatment and stitching in and around my mouth. I would be in the borstal hospital wing for the next few weeks, hardly able to consume any food other than soups or some other alternative liquid diet. If I thought I had been unfortunate then my situation was about to worsen.

In most instances of violence the usual outcome would

be for the perpetrator of any untoward behaviour to be transferred to an alternative borstal centre. This indeed was to be the fate of my assailant, but somewhere along the way the warders had misconstrued my involvement and presumed I was also involved in some ongoing turf war, and after searching my cell, they had found my makeshift weapon, thus confirming in their mind their suspicions about me. I was informed that once I had left the hospital, I would be placed in solitary confinement while they investigated the matter further. I was infuriated because I had only made the weapon as a safety measure and would have been more than happy for it never to have been produced to be used on anyone for the duration of my sentence. As always they had misinterpreted the whole situation, and although I was in fact the victim in all this, they had decided to place me on a punishment detail. I would not forget this incident for a very long while, and if it was a battle they wanted, then I would definitely oblige.

Until you have spent a period of time in solitary confinement you cannot comprehend the affect it has on you. Over the coming years I would encounter many more solitary punishment cells and I became immune to the banal existence whilst incarcerated in them. In Everthorpe everywhere I looked all the items were stored in perfect order and the floors had been scrubbed so often that they glistened and shone with a glass-like appearance. Complete silence was the order of the day, and I would not be permitted to converse in any shape or form. Should I have any requests they had to be written down and I would receive my response at a later date. Even something very trivial would take several days to be resolved. When I was out of my cell and scrubbing the floors other tasks would be found to occupy me when I was back in my cell. As the door closed behind me I would find a brand new dustbin waiting behind the door. The dustbin could have been purchased that day from any hardware store, it was that shiny and new. But its present shininess would not satisfy the warders, who had a lust for control. Accompanying the bin was a tin of metal polish and assorted rags and I was expected to polish and buff over and over and my only respite would be when one of the day's meals arrived. Should any of the warders ever look through the spy hole in the cell door and spot me being 'non-active' with the dustbin then I could be placed on yet another disciplinary charge. I would lean my arm against the bin and give the impression I was cleaning it but, in reality, I would be doing absolutely nothing to it.

When I was finally released back into regular circulation I had an attitude that would get me into a lot more trouble but, hadn't I just served a term in solitude that was unwarranted and unjustified? I promised myself that any future spell in that harsh regime of solitary would be very much deserved.

My reputation had been done no harm by the spell in solitary because most of the other boys would not relish going down there and would rarely overstep the mark in front of the warders. But for me, by now I had an aversion to anything at all authoritarian and refused to conform in any way. I would rebel at every turn and I had no inclination to toe the line. This didn't do me any favours because the troublemakers from each wing would be singled out and become renowned as 'the bad boy party' and our work duties would be far in excess of the other boys in the borstal centre.

It would be a battle of wills each day; the warders wishing to demoralise us and break our spirit, and us on the other hand, not prepared to yield even a little. It was autumn and all the leaves had fallen and the talk on the grapevine was that a novel job had been created for the bad boy party, and we were soon to discover what it entailed.

For maximum effect they had waited for a particularly cold day with a ground frost, to introduce us to our new place of employment. It was to be called 'THE BECK

PARTY' and we would be required to wear Wellington boots, albeit with the odd tear and hole in them. I can picture the warders laughing sadistically as they perforated the boots, but this would just be another challenge to my resolve.

We were marched, in long trench coats, to a series of ditches that surrounded the borstal's farm and we were instructed to break the ice on the surface and clamber down into the icy water and with the shovels we had been provided with we were to set about shovelling the leaves and other debris up and out onto the embankment. It was a meaningless and futile exercise because each day when we returned the leaves would have re-entered the brook or 'beck' as they preferred naming it. My feet would be frozen blue but I would never let the warder sense my discomfort and on the few times during these sessions we would be allowed a cigarette break I would sit on the embankment and keep my feet dangling in the cold water. My feet having acclimatised to the cold temperature of the water, I saw no reason to come out and then later re-introduce my feet to the conditions.

When I was back in the cell block, I had taken a dislike to a certain warder who revelled in his bully boy tactics. None of the boys liked him and would often say they wished that he worked on one of the other wings. I was becoming more and more of an activist and I went from cell to cell attempting to get signatures for a petition to 'out' the warder, but many chose not to sign, fearful of the warder's reputation. As for the ones that did sign, I felt I then had an obligation to attempt to bring their grievances to the attention of the house governor and so I did exactly that. It would be yet another mistake!

As each weekend approached we had what was termed outdoor pursuits which consisted of rugby, football, or cricket, and if your name appeared on a list, picked at random, for a sport you didn't wish to compete in, then there would be no alternative but to brow-beat one of the weaker boys into swapping. My name appeared on the list for rugby, a sport that I detested, but quite unusually not one boy would swap sports with me because I had found out later they had been 'advised' not to exchange. Upon arriving at the rugby field and not impressed at all, I quickly gathered that the warder in charge and actually playing with us was the object of the petition.

During the match I was made to feel the full force of some crunching tackles and accepted my fate begrudgingly, believing it would be the end of the matter, but when a later scrummage was formed with us all in the ruck searching for the ball, I was to be the recipient of a very forceful uppercut and momentarily saw stars. I had been given a very serious lesson in prison protocol and retribution. Somehow or other I thought it wise not to register any official complaint about the matter. The petition was shortly to be shelved as a very bad idea and I soon discovered that the 'pen' may not be as mighty as the 'sword' in this set of circumstances.

Violence begets violence and I was becoming very much a thorn in the warders' side. I was carefree and forever challenging the system in one way or another. I had no parental guidance or any other figurehead that I could call my own. The only visits I ever received were from the probation service, and I would think the only reason they turned up was to have a day out of the office and maybe a pleasant meal in the countryside. I had had a succession of probation officers down the years and they made such an impact on my life that I would be hard pushed to even name one of them. A profession of charlatans, if you want my opinion, as I couldn't give one example of anything that they did for me which could be described as beneficial. If anything it was the exact opposite. My dislike of the profession would culminate in me vandalising their offices one time and leading me to being given psychiatric treatment which I would continue to receive for many years.

Other boys would be coming and going from the borstal centre, either on home leave or even a final discharge from the institution, but I found myself having to stay in the place because of the probation service's failure to find me suitable accommodation. Officially I should have been out and free, but due to the maladministration of these probation officers, I would have to remain where I was for many weeks longer that I should have done.

On one occasion I was informed that nothing could be done until my 'personal' probation officer returned from her foreign holiday. No way did this government department ever have my best interests at heart and I was more than dissatisfied with the preparations for my release.

I would be like a bull in a china shop, bouncing around the landings and challenging anyone who wanted to make eye contact. I was prowling around like a caged animal. I should have been out of there ages ago, and why should I ever behave and conform? Because apparently early release for good behaviour didn't seem to apply to me, and I would always remember this fact for any future sentencing.

Let's be realistic, who would want to behave in the knowledge that your rewards would amount to little or nothing? I would never do even one sentence without finding myself in seclusion down in the punishment cells for every misdemeanour imaginable. Eventually I would be released from the borstal, but would reappear in the same institution within three months.

I was to become a resident at a local bed and breakfast hostelry in Dewsbury and it was obvious from the ages of the people in there that they had arrived here courtesy of failed marriages or some other sad circumstances, but I was a young boy for Christ's sake, and if ever there was a mismatch of sorts then this was it.

Not for the first time I felt that the probation service had been lacking in their duty of care towards me, and if they thought I would be residing here comfortably and on a regular basis then they would be sadly mistaken.

My sense of adventure (or should that be misadventure?), would soon result in me being, once again, in the back of the all too familiar police car. I would be homeless and on the streets alone, but in comparison to the shabby bed and breakfast place, I would be in my element!

CHAPTER 11

No way was I prepared to stay in the accommodation the probation service provided. It was unsuitable for someone of my tender years. I was seventeen years old and did they really think it was an adequate setting or did they simply solve their dilemma by settling for this easy option? I did have family members in the locality, but it was evident that nobody wanted to even attempt to shoulder the responsibility that went with my problematic manner.

I was under the impression there could be a possibility of me being provided with my own flat or maybe even a bed-sit, which would suffice. But instead, not for the first time, I felt let down by the probation and aftercare service. Even the term 'aftercare' rankled with me because their efforts towards me left a lot to be desired. I resented even having to attend for my weekly update reports, as they called it, because I was the person living this life and never once did I feel any progress was being made or that they were even slightly concerned about my well-being.

The probation office was situated on the fourth floor, which could be accessed by a lift. This could be stopped between floors and I would stop the lift and urinate on the floor on each visit I ever made. They would know it was me but could never prove it beyond doubt and I didn't really care how many times they confronted me about it, because on the next visit I would do the exact same thing. The angst I had towards this governmental body could never be reigned in as I hated them with a passion. I had been locked up for a long period and my punishment should have been completed, and yet I had to be monitored on a daily basis by what amounted to busybodies in my opinion, and I wanted to rebel against this at every turn.

I was aware that by leaving the bed and breakfast accommodation I would be in breach of my license conditions, and on my next appointment at the office there could be a possibility of re-arrest so it went hand-in-hand that the appointment did not take place and without intending things to get this extreme I then found myself 'on the run'.

Homeless, jobless and destitute once again, it became a feature of my life, when the reality is that I was a young boy with no direction as to how to conduct my life. Had anyone taken time out to place an arm around me and even offer me the slightest comfort then perhaps my life could have turned out much different, but it was not to be and I would always find myself alone in a sink-or-swim situation. I didn't think I was a particularly bad person. I was just given a difficult set of circumstances to deal with.

Once again I found myself out on the streets with my few personal belongings in a holdall bag, but with the added predicament of not being able to sign on at the local dole office, because obviously it was the first port of call that the local police would take to trace me.

I had reached a period in life where I was a little

fashion conscious and had recently become a skinhead with all of the accompanying accessories, i.e. sheepskin coat and a rather chic Crombie overcoat. During the day I would secret my holdall bag in bushes down by the river bank and I would retrieve it each night once darkness set in and head for the public toilets in the town centre. I felt safer in the town centre and would enter one of the cubicles and place my sheepskin coat on the floor, use my bag as a pillow, and my Crombie would afford me the warmth of a makeshift blanket. The toilets would be frequented by late night drunks on their way home after an evening's drinking in the town, and although I became scared with one incident I cannot be overly critical, because whoever did it to me would not have been aware I was only a teenage boy. I can only presume that they thought I was an older tramp who was about to be the object of their ridicule as they dragged my feet under and through the door and then set about jumping on my trailing legs until the excitement became boring and they left. I instantly recoiled and for the remainder of the night slept in a cramped-up position for fear they returned. But it had been a warning to me that I would need to acquire a safer place to rest my head.

I don't know why I hadn't thought of it before, but when I was younger I would shin down the drainpipe to the toilets of the local cinema to avoid paying to watch a film by getting through the toilet window. I now realised that the same possibility was available to me, offering me a safe haven. It would prove to be a very 'spooky' abode being as how I could hear various noises in the night as the vermin would come out to play, but all-in-all, I found it to be a very satisfactory place of rest. The added bonus of having a confectionery kiosk in the foyer which also sold cigarettes gave me great comfort in my hour of need. Obviously I would not take large amounts as I would not wish to arouse any suspicions amongst the cinema's management. Strange as it may sound I felt as though I was the cat who had the cream. I felt a sense of belonging, as if I had my own home!

Until you have been homeless you will never begin to comprehend the importance of that previous statement. I would leave the premises early in the morning each day without leaving even the slightest indication that anyone had been there.

I had tried to resist the temptation to become embroiled in any criminal activity, but as always, through a shortage of everyday funds, it became inevitable that I would need to commit further offences and so the neverending cycle continued in my criminal career. I would never try to condone even one single crime I committed, but in life sometimes it is a straightforward example of needs must.

I had decided not to burgle anywhere that was prominent or risky, and it wasn't as if I required vast amounts of money, and so I settled for doing something I hadn't done for many a year! I didn't even attend when I was officially on the register! But here I was at my old school with my gloves on my hands. On many occasions in the past, while I waited for my regular round of caning in the corridor by the headmaster's office, I had witnessed the secretary putting a red 'Elastoplast' tin, that contained the dinner tickets and money collected by the school, into a filing cabinet. I prised the filing cabinet open just enough for me to confirm that the object of my intrusion nestled comfortably amongst an assortment of papers, and I then set about prising the drawer open even further until my hand could reach in and claim my prize. I was happy with the contents, knowing it was easy money, and even though it wasn't a small fortune it would present me with a little respite.

Also in the tin were the familiar rolls of dinner tickets. I recalled angrily the times that I had stood and shamefully been given a ticket from the white roll indicating free meals while the other pupils purchased one off the blue roll. When I was at school I would often tear up that white ticket rather than have to sit amongst the sniggering asides from the well-to-do children. I would rather starve than be ridiculed by them.

After leaving the premises I set fire to the dinner tickets and therefore had nothing in my possession, should I be stopped, to link me to any crime. I could have perhaps sold the tickets to some of the older boys on my estate at a reduced rate, but after due consideration, I deemed that to be a risky enterprise. I would be up bright and early the following morning and on board a bus to Leeds to spend some of my ill-gotten gains, purchasing some new Dr Marten boots and a nice button-down Ben Sherman shirt to generally smarten up my appearance. I had also purchased a Stanley knife and attempted to convince myself that I had done so with regard to my safety, but really my violent tendencies were creeping up on me, and my anger would escalate further out of control in the coming years.

Years later I would become a much more 'balanced' individual, but at this moment in my life I had become part of a group of skinheads and we would be forever agitating and causing trouble in the predominantly Asian community. We would wear zip-up Harrington sports jackets, and on the occasions we knew we intended to cause trouble, we would turn the jackets inside out, thereby having the tartan linings on display. But after completion of any madness and mayhem we would disperse in all directions whilst returning our coats to the original mode of fashion.

I am aware, as any of them who may read this are also, of exactly who was involved in these activities, but you will appreciate that throughout this book I give no indication of the names of any individuals who may be involved in my situations. We were all hell-bent on destruction in any shape or form and my allies in these long-gone days might now be respectable businessmen or happily married, and it would not be right and proper for me to release anyone's skeletons from the cupboard!

The violence we unleashed would be excessive, and on reflection now, would be unwarranted. I was angry because of my situation and I would be out of control and not prepared to listen to anyone's advice. I was well beyond any help. I had my 'home' in the cinema, and I now was part of a group, and my sense of a sort of belonging seemed complete. We would carry our Stanley knives all the time and had no qualms about using them. I dread to dwell on the injuries we may have caused throughout this period.

Due to increased police protection in the Asian areas it quickly became apparent that we would need to get our thrills elsewhere for a while until the dust settled. We began to attend Manchester United football matches but preferred to go to the away games as the police always seemed to be unprepared for the large influx of 'fans'. There was no segregation in the early seventies, and some of the fighting was on a large scale. The main police deterrent seemed to be to confiscate people's boots, and it was hoped this would quell any trouble. I found this to be more than amusing at the time. The trouble was becoming far too high-profile, and it soon became clear that the police were concentrating their energies in and around the football ground, and so our little band of rogues would focus on alternative activities which would prove to be very rewarding. Nothing would be out of our scope. We would march into one big, well-known department store and snatch rails full of designer clothes of the day and simply march out. It would be a brave man who would attempt to stop us.

On one occasion we also dragged a till outside with us, stole the contents, and then threw the empty till back through the store window. There were no surveillance cameras in these times, and no robbery would be regarded as insurmountable. We acted as one and were fearless. If any of our exploits were of a particularly profitable nature we would leave the area at the very earliest opportunity and remain under the radar for a good while.

We would complete some very audacious robberies, and when you consider that all hooligans in those days were dressed in the exact same attire, I can imagine no police investigation that could have been more difficult than these. On many occasions we would not even attend any of the football matches. In and out. Earn a profit and get gone out of the area. My life was a little manic at this time and all of the bravado would ultimately do me no favours, as my name was getting a mention in dispatches quite often. I wasn't exactly public enemy number one but my card was marked and my days would be numbered. For the time being at least my life was a ball!!

A friend and I started to burgle chemist shops and acquire any amphetamine-based tablets we could lay our hands on. We would study pharmaceutical books in the local library and before we entered any shop. We would then have more than a good idea of exactly what would be leaving with us when we departed. The little prescription bottles that we receive on an everyday basis compare little to the very large sweet jar-like glass containers that are to be found in the rear of the shop. We would grab a few pairs of ladies tights from the front of the shop and empty the contents of the large jars into them, thus making our booty much easier to transport. We would remain awake for days on end and would sell off some of the surplus tablets to close friends. We would attend Northern Soul all-night concerts and, for a few of us, life seemed to be just one continual party!

Some of us had been involved in quite a bit of serious crime but it took a very petty and trivial incident to bring about my downfall. Along with two others I was dining at a local Chinese restaurant and as usual we would be half drunk and in high spirits, but the proprietor, eavesdropping, realised that we had no intention of paying and he had locked the door and had notified the police. My heart sank when the others were allowed to leave after agreeing to settle their bill but I was to be held once again in custody while my recent mini crime wave was to be investigated. I would shortly be detained and find myself missing the next four seasons!

CHAPTER 12

I knew I could not expect any favourable report from my probation officer as I had not exactly toed the line so obviously no application for bail would be presented. I would find myself at Thorpe Arch Remand Centre in Wetherby again although this time I would be a very cocksure individual being as how I had been through the system before and knew exactly what to expect in comparison to the new recruits in the reception area, whose faces were filled with dread.

I was familiar with every procedure, and it's a sad reflection on my life that already at the age of seventeen I seemed to be a little institutionalised. Nothing fazed me anymore and whereas other internees would have had the incentive of early release dates should their good behaviour merit it, none of that applied to me, so I had no need to conform to rules and regulations. I would constantly find myself in lots of disciplinary procedures because I just fell into that pattern. Once any situation had become a battle of wills then I would go the extra mile every time. I hated the establishment and all that it represented.

Because of my age I had already leap-frogged the judicial system, having been the youngest inmate at my borstal centre on the first occasion, so the only sentence available to the court would be to give me a second term of borstal training. In effect I had been set a sort of catch-up procedure, bringing me back into line and where I should actually be. But where would the fear factor be? There was nothing they could put in front of me for the next twelve months that I hadn't encountered before.

Not one thing had changed with the previous procedure and I was sent to Armley Prison in Leeds for a period of two weeks and then transferred to Strangeways Prison, to the borstal wing, in Manchester.

Strangeways had the most fearsome reputation of any prison throughout the country. No regime ever took advantage of its prisoners as much as this one did, and although it would be a long time coming, the uprising of the eighties and the ongoing riot would be long overdue as the world's media witnessed our country's worst ever revolt. The prison and its warders would be barbaric, and many an inmate was beaten to within an inch of their lives.

It was wise to try and keep one's head down whilst an inmate here, but in typical fashion I fell foul of what the warders classed as their strict code of conduct. We would be given a razor blade each morning to shave any stubble that was visible, but I felt that the hair on my head was growing too much and so took it upon myself to shave it all from my head. When the cell door was reopened I would be expected to return the blade as it would be required to use the following morning.

It took me by surprise when the landing warder rang the alarm bell and every available officer came rushing to the source of the alarm and I was placed in a restraint position and frog-marched down to solitary confinement. My 'crime' apparently was one of self-inflicting wounds with the impromptu haircut. I kid you not, and foolishly expecting that the governor would give me a sympathetic hearing was another rash misjudgement on my part. I was to serve seven days in solitary and would be expected to place all of my bedding and possessions outside of my cell each morning until late evening. Thus throughout the day I was permitted nothing except a table and chair at which to eat that day's food.

The warders at this jail would take no prisoners (pardon the pun!) and it gave me great pleasure when it was practically razed to the ground. They were complacent and arrogant and believed they would always rule with an iron fist.

With the demise of the old Strangeways prison I now have to give a little praise to the new prison that rose from the ashes because all I ever hear now is favourable reports, especially in respect of the educational facilities. I served my time in confinement and to be quite truthful sometimes I preferred the peace and solitude down there. In any prison establishment the one way above any other to escape the overcrowding in the regular prison quarters would be to have a spell in solitary. Something I would manage to do all through the years at every prison I was locked up in.

Because of my refusal to conform to authority and toe the line I found myself at Strangeways for the next four months, awaiting allocation to my Borstal Centre. It was obvious that my series of tests, as previously, would result in me being sent to Everthorpe in Hull once again but the authorities still insisted that I sit the tests. Some of the tests would be quite comical, as I would be examined to determine if I was colour blind! How on earth that gives some sort of indication as to which borstal is suitable is beyond me. The reason I am critical of the amount of time spent in Strangeways being assessed is because it is classed as 'dead time'. The actual sentence does not begin until the very first day of arrival at the Borstal Centre.

But, as expected, Everthorpe was once again to become my hall of residence and it would hold no fears for me. Because of my previous bad behaviour on my earlier sentence I was given a cell on the first floor, close to the warders office, giving them the opportunity to monitor my movements more closely. Other inmates on this landing consisted of informants and reviled paedophiles and rapists. If anyone thought I was going to settle in and make new 'friends' they would be way off the mark.

It had been brought to my attention that a certain inmate 'living' directly opposite from my cell was a serious 'sex case' and each time his cell door would be opened he would be very hesitant about venturing out to associate with the other boys. These sorts of inmates would attempt to convince you that they are detained for other 'acceptable' crimes such as burglary, but their nervous actions would give them away. In many instances the warders would bring to our attention just what offence the inmates were in for, and then make themselves busy with other duties at the opposite end of the landing, in effect giving a 'green light' for me to mete out a little rough justice on him.

I followed this individual into the washroom area and quickly placed a pillowslip over his head so that he could not identify me at a later stage. I had earlier placed a heavy PPQ battery into a sock and then smashed it in the facial area of the pillowslip until it turned red and his body went limp. I then let him fall to the floor. I then quickly exited the washroom and made for the TV room, where other inmates would readily confirm that I had been there for quite a while, thereby ensuring my alibi. Upon making my way back to my cell I was able to witness the 'sex case' being stretchered to the hospital in a very bloodied and dazed state.

Not all warders are in agreement with these sorts of actions and retribution but, for the ones who are, I commend your principles. In later chapters I will slash one miscreant badly and I will also scald one with hot boiling water and sugar.

If any of you recoil at these stories I can assure you that I never lost a minute's sleep over my actions. Many of these people are predatory animals and many a parent of a young child that has been affected by their deeds would welcome the opportunity to stand over their child's attacker.

To any parents out there who have been dissatisfied with the lenient sentencing of our judicial system could I give you a little comfort by assuring you that when any 'decent criminal' gets even the slightest chance to inflict pain on these people, not one of us hesitates to leave our mark on them. Literally. Obviously I would expect there to be readers amongst you who would regard this particular type of violence to be very excessive, but I lived in the 'jungle' and amongst we animals and such, this was the order of the day. How would any of you react had it been your children affected?

It also gave me the added bonus of being in favour with the warder who had given me the task of dealing with the paedophile, and so throughout my stay I would never find myself in an unfavourable situation with him, and I could imagine he would tell his other warder friends, over the odd pint of beer, that I was a reliable lad to be trusted to carry out a task. It is maybe the one thing that warders and prisoners have all had in common and that is our dislike of paedos. I should have been concerned for the way my violent tendencies seemed to have become second nature, but I gave it no thought at all, and if anything, I would be the first in the queue for any proposed assault.

I was given the job of scrubbing the large dining hall along with twenty others. We would need to place all the chairs on the tables and scrub right the way through three times each day after each meal sitting had taken place. On completion of our task we would be permitted to sit down and 'hide' at the rear of the dining hall whilst waiting for the floor to dry. With the chairs on the tables hiding us from view we would tell each other crime related anecdotes until this became boring and we then invented a game whereby all of our names would be placed in a hat and the two names drawn out would have to have a three-minute round of bare-knuckle fighting with each other. I can laugh now at some of the mismatches that took place but it most certainly taught us how to fight, and getting the odd black eye or even a fat lip would surface, but I never saw it as 'bullying' as such.

I was transferred to another work detail that required us to polish and buff all the main corridors in and around the chapels within the borstal, but I only lasted four days as I foolishly found myself on a disciplinary charge and placed in solitary confinement yet again.

It had not taken me long to discover the communal wine inside one of the chapels and I gladly set about having my first taste of alcohol for perhaps eight months, and it soon became apparent that I had done so. I was taken under escort to the punishment cells and whilst being placed in my cell observed that the shiniest dust bins in the whole of the galaxy were still available to be given yet another polishing.

Most misdemeanours in institutions would be dealt with by way of a seven-day exclusion but the governor took great exception to my sacrilegious offence and doubled my stay to fourteen days. All I would be permitted in my cell in solitary, from early morning until late at night, would be my table and chair and a jug of water to go with my plastic mug. One of the warders would challenge me to turn the water into wine, which I thought was quite comical.

All solitary punishment blocks are run with the same set of standards, and once you have become accustomed to the silence and boredom factors, then one day is just like any other. Time still goes by and that is the one thing warders cannot prevent from happening.

After I was released back into the normal prison population I was given yet another job but this one had the tag name 'shit detail' and involved exactly that. While inmates were locked down throughout the night and therefore had no access to the toilet, other than a chamber pot in the corner of the cell, they would take the option if needed to defecate onto newspaper laid on the floor of the cell. It was then wrapped into a tight paper parcel and thrown outside as far away from your own cell window as possible. My new task would be to pull an open-backed cart around and shovel up all of the offending parcels and place them in the cart. The job would become increasingly difficult should there have been any rain throughout the night that would release the contents. In my own sick thought process I felt as though I had been 'shit-shovelling' my whole life so nothing had changed here then! It was about this time that the only incident that ever presented me with a favourable outcome whilst in any prison, took place.

Overcrowding in prisons and borstals had become unmanageable and the ways and means of giving out early releases by way of reduced sentences had begun to take place. We were summoned to the main assembly hall to be addressed by the governor who informed us that, rather than our sentence starting from the first day we arrived in the borstal, it would now be amended to the actual day that the sentence was passed in court. I was dumbstruck and thought it must be some sort of practical joke, but after a reassuring discussion with my House Master, I skipped to my cell safe in the knowledge I had just gained an additional six months off my sentence and I would be due some form of home leave within a month.

If it came as a shock to me then it had most certainly done the same with my probation officer on the outside, who very quickly had to put contingency plans into place. The new release plans would not be forthcoming and, as on so many occasions before, I would find myself incarcerated for a longer period than I needed to be due to their complete incompetence. Me and the probation service were about to embark on a collision course that would conclude with me being placed in a mental asylum.

CHAPTER 13

It was good to be out of the prison, although once again, I found myself residing in a shabby bed and breakfast, from which we were all expected to vacate on completion of the morning meal and not expected to return until late evening, thereby giving the landlady time to supposedly change the bedding and have a general tidy around.

I had met a girl I shall call Sandra, and we would meet up regularly throughout the following weeks. On one particular cold day she decided to take me home to her parents' abode because she knew they would be out and we could perhaps have a little privacy. After having had a few drinks I enquired where the bathroom was and as I made my way along the corridor. A little old lady waved in my direction so when I got back to Sandra I informed her that I thought I had just seen her grandmother. She then told me that her parents ran the house by way of a nursing home for the elderly. I pretended to take little interest but my mind was already racing, believing there could be a possibility of some prescription drugs in the home.

In a situation where there are elderly people you have to appreciate that they sleep very little, if indeed they sleep at all, and so there was more than likely a great many barbiturate sleeping tablets to be found. I discovered it was just as I had imagined when I came across a dispensary cabinet in the kitchen. I thought I had struck the jackpot but the next six months would prove to be a catastrophic period of my life, for I developed an addiction for the first time ever and this resulted in me having two very near-death experiences.

Throughout my whole life I have always taken a liking to any drug that heightens awareness and provides additional energy, and yet there I was, addicted to Turinal, a synthetic steroid, which was a very strong sedative. Try as I may I could not break the habit and I would wake up regularly with black eyes and be informed that I had been in fights and situations that I could not recall. Most of my days and nights would be spent in total confusion and on one occasion I was found slumped in the yard of a friend of mine, and he had needed to roll me about in a patch of wet grass and then drive me to the local hospital, slapping me continually across the face until a doctor could inject me with adrenaline to speed up my heart rate.

I would not know what I had done from one day to the next, but apparently on one drug-fuelled binge I had gone to the local probation office and smashed a few windows and thrown the furniture about. I will not deny this must have taken place but I could not remember any involvement and it was obvious the sleeping tablets had become a big problem in my life. I no longer had ready access to the nursing home after I had shown up there in a semi-conscious state and Sandra's parents had forbidden her to see me again. I would find myself on the slippery slope with the prospect of having to burgle a chemist's shop again to fuel my habit, unless I accepted the proposals set in place to put me into the local mental asylum.

I was to be treated at Stores Hall Mental Institution on the outskirts of Huddersfield and I can honestly say, hand on heart, that I would never again come across such a dreadful place – it almost destroyed me.

You may feel that calling a place an asylum would be politically incorrect, but I can assure you that, if any place was ever deserving of the title, then this place was the one! I was placed on a long ward together with maybe thirty others and each of us was being treated for various mental issues. Upon arrival I was given pyjamas and a dressing gown and informed that, in a week's time, after it was assessed that I was not likely to be a danger to any members of the public, then I would be permitted to wear my own clothes. The longer I remained at the hospital, the more it became clear that some of the patients would be constantly clad in their pyjamas, so this warned me that they had very strong issues and would need to be avoided at all costs.

Stores Hall, as in many mental homes, was a very controlled and subdued environment and many of us would have the drug Lorgactyl administered to us, which was the most potent tranquiliser available at that time. It was used frequently within our prisons and a way and means of controlling troublesome prisoners, and would be injected into the soles of the feet to immobilise the central nervous system in an instant.

Here in Stores Hall it would be done in a more 'humane' way and we would be injected in our buttocks each day, although at the time, I was not aware of what medication I was being given or the likely effects. The whole place had such a lethargic aura about it and most patients could barely comprehend what anyone was saying, and the same would apply to their own attempts at speech. I witnessed patients masturbating each other on the ward and I cursed myself for so readily agreeing to undertake this voluntary treatment process. I felt that because I had no parental concern in my background, the authorities simply had free reign to do whatever they wished with me. Of course it gave me the impetus to beat my addiction, but surely there was a safer environment than this one to do it in. Because I was a voluntary patient I had been allowed to wear my own clothes, but a lot of the other patients had been sectioned by the courts to be treated, and in many instances some had been 'sectioned' for a course lasting just six months, but had in fact been there for many years and would possibly be there for many more to come.

Everything was geared towards medication and I resembled a zombie in the manner in which I walked around. Even the simplest tasks would become increasingly difficult. There were classes during the day under the term 'Occupational Therapy' and we would all be encouraged to attend and become involved in the activities. We did attend, but found ourselves going to sleep at the tables very often.

The hospital was set in a couple of acres of ground in a very picturesque area, which also consisted of a newsagent's and other shops and, very surprisingly, a public house. The pub was for visitors to socialise in more than anything else, and perhaps for the use of members of staff.

The hospital was on a very busy bus route and there were various stops situated throughout the grounds for transporting people to and from the hospital. I was not comfortable with my surroundings one bit and made a mental note of the schedules of the buses going down into Huddersfield town centre. How I had landed myself in this dreadful situation was beyond me. I was still a teenager and found myself amongst some of the craziest people imaginable. The only thing missing, it seemed, was Jack Nicholson and a boat. This place really was like *One Flew Over the Cuckoo's Nest*, yet much more so.

One fellow patient spoke of nothing but fishing, and it seemed to be his only passion in life. I told him I had come across a small brook on my walkabouts in the hospital grounds, which I was permitted to do, and he enquired whether there were any fish in the brook. He became animated even just discussing the water and the fish, and so it led me to sneaking him off the ward and away in the direction of the stream. As we came across the banks of the water he began wailing and screaming like a banshee, and so I left him in his excited state and wandered back.

As I neared the hospital I became aware of emergency sirens blaring and the ward about to be placed in a state of lockdown. Little did I realise it involved the disappearance of our friendly neighbourhood fisherman who posed a significant threat to the public at large. Maybe I should have realised, because he was clothed in his dressing gown, that there was a problem with him, or maybe I just didn't care because it had broken up the monotony of the day.

He was located in next to no time and, as fishing folklore goes, he most definitely wasn't 'the one that got away'. My involvement in the matter soon became clear to members of staff and I knew that my days would be numbered, although I was soon to make the decision for them. Who wants to be pushed when you can quite easily jump yourself?

I no longer craved my addiction to sleeping tablets and I had eaten well for the past five weeks and managed to save a little money from my benefits, which I hadn't needed to touch. I would be expected to take oral medication in the form of Valium tablets, but I would secret these in the well of my mouth beneath my tongue, until such time as I could flush them down the toilet.

I was a voluntary patient and could leave at any time, but I had a sneaky suspicion that the probation officer would object to this at such an early stage, and so my decision would be to leave in my own time, but attempt to clear my body of some of the medication at least. Within a few days I felt much more lucid and my judgement seemed less impaired than it had been. I informed one of the ward nurses that I needed some essentials from the hospital shop, and that I would return shortly, all the time knowing that I was about to board one of the buses into the town centre. I had no reason to be concerned about what I was about to do because I was safe in the knowledge that, for a change, I would not be a wanted fugitive by the hospital. I would probably have problems with the probation service but that would be nothing new and I would deal with that at a later stage.

I felt a great sorrow for some of the patients as I boarded the bus because I knew that some of them would remain in this hospital for many more years yet, but having said that, they knew of nothing else, and maybe they preferred remaining in the sanctity of the hospital instead of the prospect of the bustle of everyday life outside.

But I had made my mind up to seek pastures new before the time came when maybe a patient decided he would like to masturbate me. Not my cup of tea at all I'm afraid!

I felt a great sense of relief the further I was away from the hospital and although I felt very docile for the next few days, I soon returned to functioning normally. 'Normally' for me seemed to centre around homelessness and a life on the streets. The next few weeks centred around me sleeping in derelict houses but, if only for a short time, my fortunes were about to change.

A lady who has since died became my saviour. The woman in question was called Jackie Quinn-Frost and even though she had three children, she accepted me as one of her own and she became my second mum and could see no wrong in me.

In later years she formed an action group to rescue

youngsters with addictions and she became a well-known personality in a small area close to Dewsbury. It broke my heart to be informed that she died last year, but I was pleased to hear that her funeral cortege brought the whole area to a standstill. She would be a saint to many over the years, but at this particular moment she had discovered my plight, and made it her mission to come and find me to provide me with a home. This lady knew nothing of my background or my latest history, but took it upon herself to try to improve my life and I could never ever thank her enough.

Until her demise last year I had maintained contact with her for forty years or more and I could never express how much she meant to me or the debt of gratitude I owe her.

God bless you, Jackie Quinn-Frost.

I found myself in a very comfortable and loving home and Jackie's own children didn't have the slightest objection about me being there. I had near enough everything that I had ever lacked before and, with hindsight, it should have been the turning point in my life, but I suppose the seeds had long been sown and I had a violent and disturbed personality. Jackie assumed all responsibility for me and notified the probation service that I would now be living with her and her family. In no way could I describe how good that sense of belonging felt to me after all that I had been through. I even managed to get a few paid jobs along the way, now that I had a stable home life, but the pay was never enough and it would be many years before I could deal with the situation of being told what to do. I had never had a taste of adapting to the real world and its responsibilities and I struggled. Jackie would console me each time I told her that I had lost another job but she would never berate me too much. She understood me and my complexities better than anyone before or since. I tested her patience on many an occasion but would still be greeted with a warm embrace.

I had only lived at Jackie's for a few months and after an evening out on the town I got involved in an argument at the local taxi rank over something as petty as to who the next taxi for hire belonged to. The altercation got so out of hand that I cut my aggressor on his cheek with the knife I had taken from my sock, which resulted in me being arrest for assault.

It was as if I couldn't come to terms with any semblance of order in my life, and I would shortly find myself in a young offenders prison serving a six-month sentence. Although Jackie scolded me for what I had done she assured me that I would always have a bed waiting in her home when I got out. She would open her home to me on many more occasions!

CHAPTER 14

So there I was again, back in my familiar surroundings and on the landing in Armley Prison in Leeds awaiting transportation to Strangeways in Manchester. The only difference here being that I was now classed as capable of doing the same tasks as the adult population of the jail and I would be sewing mail bags all day long.

The requirement was that I would need to sew six stitches to the inch on the canvas bag – that was inside and out – and I would need to complete two full bags a day to earn the princely sum of three pounds per week. Should any of us take a bag up for inspection and the stitching be below standard, the officer in charge would simply cut all of the stitching away and hand you back the bag to begin the whole procedure again, therefore costing you a whole morning's work and leaving you short on wages and, in turn, short of money for purchasing tobacco. Never has there been a more soul-destroying job or could there ever be again. My fingers were blistered and sore.

The bags, on completion, would need marking with what was called 'Tailor's Chalk' and we would steal little amounts to smuggle back onto the wing together with a big sewing needle. In the evenings, once the warders had gone home, we would dilute the chalk with water and make different coloured inks and set about tattooing each other with some very abstract designs. To this day my arms and hands are covered in homemade tattoos and some of them are of a very silly nature and very much regretted now.

I even have my National Insurance number inked in along my knuckles, which seemed quite funny at the time, but not so today.

We were interned on our own landing, which was set aside for young prisoners or 'Y.P.s' as we were called, and it quickly became clear that the stern format we would have endured in detention centres and borstals would not be the order of the day here. Yes, some form of regimentation still had to exist, but the warders would have presumed that, being as how the short sharp shock treatment had not served its purpose, what would be the point of being forceful and heavy-handed?

In earlier instances, statistics on detention centres and borstals would maybe have informed you that a third of inmates had not reoffended, nor would they be likely to. But for the ones such as ourselves, still in the system, there was a less likely chance of us being rehabilitated and so the warders realised this and had a softer approach.

In the workshop we would sit on a long row of seats with a long piece of wood running all the way through to bind the chairs together, therefore preventing the chairs becoming ready-made weapons should any disturbance take place. We were expected to complete two full mail bags each and every day, and no excuse would be tolerated from the workshop managers, who had a different agenda to the warders and had production targets to meet.

Whenever we went for meal breaks or exercise on the yard we would put our initials in chalk on the uncompleted bags and place them under our chair to be completed sometime later. A big bonus was that any new prisoners coming in would not be aware of this procedure and place their bag under the seat without marking it, and the more experienced boys would circle like vultures to purloin the half or nearly completed bag as soon as the owner was out of sight. These stolen bags would be retrieved at a later date and passed off as one of our own and that gave us the chance to add to our set targets by having done additional work, or just to sit about talking and doing nothing with the time that we had managed to save!

You must never believe the old adage about there being honour amongst thieves, or at least, it never applied here.

It would cause great amusement witnessing the victims searching again and again in the spot where they believed they had left it, and it wasn't as if there was a Neighbourhood Watch scheme in the mailbag shop. We had all come through the system in the same way that a young footballer comes through every academy until finally making the grade. We had graduated, and knew every trick in the book. Even Fagin in Oliver Twist would have been proud of this bunch.

I was promoted to landing cleaner and had many extra perks and spin-offs, but I would also create some of my own and resort to a little subterfuge with whichever warder was on duty each night. I was given the opportunity to empty my chamber pot first while the big sluice would be empty of faeces and urine, and so less smelly. When the warder was not looking I would wedge a scrubbing brush with a floor cloth wrapped around it tightly down the plug hole and, as the occupants of each cell came in turn the build-up and the stench would be inevitable. My cell door would remain open throughout this 'slopping-out' period in case any of the prisoners needed certain items that I was responsible for handing out. Finally, once the landing had all been done, the warder had to move up or down to one of the other landings and complete the same process; he would come to lock my door last of all. After checking all of his last-minute details he would come to my door and apologetically inform me that the sluice was completely full and blocked up, and state that he knew it was a dirty task for me to have to undertake, but if I managed to empty it all satisfactorily he would notify whichever warder was on TV association duty that I would be coming down for a little television viewing, to which I was not normally entitled. He would depart, wishing me luck under the misguided belief that I would be elbow deep in shit and urine. Little did he know that I had a small piece of wire which enabled me to fiddle about gently until it made contact with the cloth surrounding the brush, and with a gentle tug I was able to pull the 'blockage' out and wait a polite period of time before making my way down to watch some television. It would be different warders on the landings most nights and so the trick could be applied on numerous occasions, and I can assure you, I took full advantage.

Doing a six-month sentence at this time meant I needed to complete two-thirds of my sentence, and I would get a third off for good behaviour, and, as I had already served a month or so, I would have thought that I could have served out my sentence in Leeds being as how I had little time left to serve. However, due to overcrowding and cell space being needed I once again found myself on my way to my least favourite prison – Strangeways in Manchester.

The warders here constantly gave you a hard time and made your sentence unbearable, although I had the comfort of knowing that it would only be for a short time. The majority of the prisoners would consist of Mancunians and Scousers from Liverpool with an attitude, and in the company of these people one needs to learn to keep one's head down and hide away from the crowd.

I would at least be receiving regular mail from Jackie, although she could not afford the travel costs to Manchester to visit me. So for once I felt at least someone had my best interests at heart, and it soon brings home the importance of something as small as getting a letter and news of the outside world, however trivial that information may be.

The work detail once again turned out to be of a very menial nature and one workshop would have prisoners screwing a never-ending supply of screws of varying sizes into electrical household plugs. But my workshop was less demanding, and a toy soldier production line was in operation. One prisoner would be required to paint all of the soldiers' shields a royal blue or red, and then pass these to the next person who would need to paint a sword or a rifle a different colour. This would go on and on until each soldier was complete and then another prisoner's job would be to insert them into the packaging that would hold full battalions or platoons of men.

In some way I suppose that the Home Office regarded this as rehabilitating therapy, but knowing what I know now, if I was to have a bet, I'm sure there would have been some form of profit margin involved and we were no more than just cheap labour.

Strangeways was a big, sprawling prison with a complete prison for adults and a prison within a prison for borstal boys and young prisoners. In the midst of it all stood a very tall tower which had in fact been the hanging tower, used regularly until the abolition of hanging in the 50s. We would walk in its shadow each day while we had our daily exercise and it would send shivers down me, being aware of its morbid past.

We were allowed one hour's exercise each day,

although, should it rain, it would be deemed 'inclement weather' and no exercise would be permitted that day. Until you have lived in Manchester none of you could even begin to realise just how much rainfall Manchester gets. It's like an Indian monsoon once the rain comes as it continues day after day, and the population of Manchester may get accustomed to it, but to the inmates of the prison, it means weeks at a time without seeing any daylight, and each of us would have a very ashen-faced look about us.

It was with this look I found myself discharged early one morning and began making my way towards the Manchester Exchange Railway Station for my trans-Pennine connection back to my beloved Yorkshire. I still had not seen the last of Strangeways as I would return yet again within two years, and in a severe disciplinary manner the next time. But for now I could let the place see my skinny posterior heading in a completely different direction!

CHAPTER 15

It only takes a thirty-minute train journey to reach Dewsbury from Manchester, and I was soon back in my home town. As promised Jackie had a room ready and waiting for me and even considering I was a very nasty and violent-minded individual, she would always remain tolerant towards me. For many years I would be made welcome at three different homes with Jackie and her three young children and she would always try her best to redirect me.

At this time, upon my release, she was living on Moorside Road, Dewsbury Moor. An estate which in later years would gain worldwide notoriety due to the Shannon Matthews murder case. A small girl was abducted by her own mother and boyfriend and hidden in the loft, whilst all of the neighbourhood and police searched for her.

Dewsbury Moor was and still is a typical northern housing estate, but with a very tight-knit community, and I enjoyed living on this estate much more than the neighbouring estate where I grew up in my childhood.

I was encouraged by Jackie to seek work and I eventually found work in a rag warehouse named Plaistere and Hangers in Revensthorpe, not far away. All of the employees had some sort of 'track record' or other and so there was no need for me to feel apprehensive that my own coloured past would inhibit my progress. Life was good for a change and I settled in to the stability that a good home and work life brought to me. Finally I would be leading a very honest and upstanding existence. I would be well-fed and looked after by my adoptive mum and I would have money to spend on my favourite passion, which was buying clothes to keep up with whatever the fashion was at that particular time.

I had been a skinhead and a suedehead with all of the sharp clothes of the time, and would often be seen in two-tone suits and a little pork pie hat on my head and royal brogues or loafers on my feet, with lots of segs nailed into the bottom of the leather soles which would make a loud tap dancing sound. After all, what's the point of looking sharp if people can't see you coming? The noise made by the segs would soon herald your arrival.

Jay Tex, Brutus or Ben Sherman button-down collars were the shirts of the day, and most definitely very bright lucid socks which, looking back, would have appeared quite garish, but back in the day I took a great deal of pride in my appearance and I would strut about like a peacock. I had a selection of suits and one of my favourites would be a Prince of Wales checked one, and I would swagger around like I owned the estate whilst I wore it and with a very chic Crombie coat I would be looking more like Arthur Daly in *Minder* than a recently released felon. I had some semblance of order back in my life, but then a certain mode of fashion surfaced and brought my earlier violent tendencies to the fore like a tsunami.

Stanley Kubrick had just released the most controversial film entitled *A Clockwork Orange* and I became obsessed with it from the very first moment I viewed it – I could recite the first chapter of the book word for word. To this day the characters, Alex, Pete, Georgie and Dim have remained with me, along with the Moloko Plus substance that they drank that had initiated their violence.

My sharp sense of dress was to be replaced by some long white baker's trousers and my Dr Martens boots would resurface as a fashion accessory and I would also sport, what became synonymous with the movie, the half set of false eyelashes, and on reflection, I may have looked quite silly but in my own mind at the time, I had pulled off and mastered the look. Had it simply remained in the fashion-conscious sphere all would have been well and good, but I craved for the violent activities and the outrage that the film caused, and this just fuelled my own fire.

There would be copycat violence throughout the country, culminating in many cinemas refusing to screen the movie, but that was too late in my case as I had viewed it twice and had read the paperback book continuously. I had always been violent-natured and now my psychotic urges had been rekindled and it would lead to my downfall once again.

Jackie constantly tried to get to the bottom of anything that was troubling me as it would be impossible not to notice that my mainly-white clothing was constantly blood-stained from whatever situation I had been involved in that night. It was difficult for me to open up, although I would try my best to assure her that she was in no way responsible or should feel she was at fault. She had her own problems to contend with being as how her long standing partner, Dick Frost, was due to be discharged from Preston prison at any time and I understood her concerns and promised to correct my behaviour, which proved easier said than done.

When I had stayed at Jackie's previously Dick had been in prison, and had never actually even met me. She was concerned that he may disagree with me staying in the family home and she wanted to break it to him gently. This period was in the days when public houses used to close at three o'clock in the afternoon and re-open again at 5.30 p.m. because licensing hours were very strict and limited. However, for people in the know, it would be quite possible to drink at clubs where people would have staggered shifts, such as bus workers and railway workers, who would have their own social clubs and they would be permitted to take in a guest and therefore, if we had the available funds, we could drink throughout the day and into the night. Should the local rugby league team in Dewsbury be playing at home, the clubhouse had a bar which served early until late throughout the game and it was on one of these long all-day drinking binges that I committed one of the silliest and costliest crimes of my career.

I had ventured out in my customary attire in the *Clockwork Orange* mode and drank very heavily throughout the day, commencing at the local hall for seasoned veterans of previous conflicts and military personnel of the day, where we could purchase alcohol from ten in the morning. My friends and I would mingle outside until any old gentleman would agree to sign us in on the pretext that we were 'related'. In return we would need to purchase our 'grandfather' a few drinks. By the time we made our way to the rugby ground intending to purchase more at the bar I was very intoxicated and in high spirits, but as per usual, when I was in this state I would be of a violent disposition and very aggressive.

The police had caught me on a few occasions in the past carrying a knife, resulting in them being presented with the simple task of charging me with being in possession of an offensive weapon, whereas, had I not had the knife, I would have been free to go. So the lesson had been learnt and I now carried a long-handled steel comb and the handle had been sharpened on a grinding stone wheel at my place of work – it proved to be more than an adequate weapon but also, quite innocently, a means of combing my hair should the police get inquisitive.

Nearing the ground in my drunken state, I stopped a man who I believed to be a stranger and asked him to give me a cigarette. He replied that he did not smoke and so I suggested in a threatening manner that it may be wise for him to give me some money to buy some. He became defensive, claiming he had no money as he attempted to retreat away from me. Had I not been as drunk as I was I would have heard him call me by my Christian name, but I did not hear him, or the outcome could have been a lot different. Instead I had rounded on my prey and brought him to the ground, and in the same motion brought my 'tail comb' round and drew blood from his upper arm area whilst assuring him there would be more to come if he did not comply. I went through his pockets and I should have listened to his earlier claims of having none as, despite my continual efforts, I had managed to locate no more than two shillings in pre-decimal money in his pockets. One of my friends hauled me off the ailing man and as we made our escape the man's threats to have me arrested rang in my ears.

I ran away, believing it would be difficult to pin the assault on me, but I would find out at a later date that I had worked at a factory with the man and he knew me personally. How could I have been so stupid? I cursed my own stupidity and the fruits of my reward (two shillings) would be scant compensation, being the paltry sum it was. The police insisted we go through the formalities of an identification parade, after they had arrested me at a later date, in order to make their case even more water-tight. I had been involved in quite a few instances of violence that they were aware of, but had not been able to prove, and they wanted me off the streets. Now I had given them the satisfaction of simplifying their task.

I was granted bail even though the police had objected strongly to it, and I'm sure every single criminal will tell you that in these circumstances the option available is to make your anticipated spell in prison a profitable one while you can. I was a condemned man. A man walking the streets committing robberies with violence would not be treated lightly in those days, and there would be no doubt that I would be going to prison. It was simply a question of for how long. I had sworn to myself on an earlier occasion that I would not go behind a cell door again unless a profit margin was involved, and yet there I was, staring a lengthy sentence in the face for the sake of a few shillings. I would need to rectify that while I was on bail and set about plundering anything that was not nailed down to compensate for my recent sad efforts. I did not know how to drive a car and so would find myself focusing all my energies in and around Dewsbury. Until, that is, Jackie's 'husband' Dick was released from prison, and it quickly became clear that he also was a career criminal who would very quickly fall in to his usual selfsame pattern of reoffending.

Don't get me wrong. Most prisoners who come out of any jail have all the best intentions in the world of adjusting back into society and securing gainful employment, but for a variety of different reasons the dream and desire never materialise and inevitably crime and the lure of easy money seem much more attainable. Hence Dick became our driver, and we would embark on a series of office and shop burglaries.

For all of Jackie's fears, if anything, Dick had taken me as a father would to a son and we would go out most evenings foraging for any possible earner, or 'on the mooch' as he preferred to call it. It was a strange pairing, but him being the elder, it would permit me to be trained in the skills of entering premises a little less noisily than I had done previously. I would watch in quiet admiration whilst he 'hot-wired' any vehicle that we would be borrowing for that night, and he became my tutor in a lot of respects. I had nothing to fear regarding capture at any time as my robbery case had already been sent and committed to Leeds Crown Court and I was marking time until my sentence.

We went to an office block in Huddersfield which I had burgled many years before when I had myself a nice little earner by way of a little ready cash that had been left about. On this occasion the rewards would be significantly higher, as to our total amazement we discovered the safe had been locked and secured for the night, albeit with the bunch of keys left on top of the safe. Initially we thought that the keys would belong to some other section of the building and would have nothing to do with the safe in front of us. But on trying a few keys and hearing that click which allows access to the door, we moved the handle and could not hide our unbridled excitement. It may not seem to be an overly excessive amount of money, but we stuffed the best part of two thousand pounds sterling and several hundred pounds worth of traveller's cheques into our pockets, content in knowing we could live the high life for the next few weeks.

This find would act as overdue compensation for the burglary a few weeks previously when we had been given 'reliable information' that a local haulage company, due to a fire, was continuing their business from a few portable cabins in the yard adjacent to the burnt building. The rumour was that, due to drivers arriving back at base from all over Europe at different times of the week, there would be many pay packets on hold within one of the portacabins. It all sounded very feasible, and so we set off on yet another little adventure that would become the hardest night's work I would ever be involved in.

Upon entering the office area, Dick and I came across a rather heavy safe, thus seeming to confirm that the whispers may indeed be correct and monies would be due. We rocked the safe from side to side and could hear what sounded like loose change falling around. We would presume now, greedily, that where there is change there would also be bank notes. After several attempts to gain access without any joy and with the realisation that time would be against us shortly, we took the decision to move the car as close as we possibly could and take the safe away with us.

This proved to be a very laborious task as we would need to tumble the safe over and over down some railway sidings for a distance of perhaps 500 yards to a secluded spot where we had parked the car. We transported it back to our home and at our own leisure now, we spent the evening chiselling and hammering and baling-out what seemed to be a never-ending stream of sawdust. We had now been 'on-the-job' for almost eleven hours when we made our first breakthrough and high-fived each other, only to discover that the sound of the 'loose change' was in actual fact a few sets of keys, and the rest of the contents consisted of not a lot more than paperwork and work schedules.

To Jackie's displeasure the safe remained in her kitchen for the next few days until we finally mustered up some additional strength to take it in the car and roll it down the canal embankment into the water, never to be seen again, thankfully.

In between doing burglaries in the evenings, I would be prone to 'earning a living' during the day by whatever means were at my disposal, and I had begun to perfect a little scam in the local public toilets in the town centre. However, I should have realised that I had executed this scheme too often and my 'career' and my freedom along with it, would be coming to a very untimely end.

I would loiter about in the toilets, pretending to urinate, until such time when some unsuspecting gentleman would go behind one of the doors into a cubicle to relieve himself by other means. My victim would need to be a well-dressed individual with an overcoat, more often than not, but a suit would suffice so long as the victim was wearing braces, which would require him to remove his jacket. After a short interlude I would enter the neighbouring cubicle and standing on the seat, reach over, and in an instant, snatch the coat hung up on the back of the door and be on my way out of the toilets. The victim would be so taken aback, considering he would still need to fulfil his bodily function, that I had gone before it even registered with him that he had not only lost his coat but the wallet that lay therein.

I set about following the selfsame procedure on another victim and all seemed to be going according to plan, until I bolted from my own cubicle straight into the arms of a waiting undercover police officer.

There was to be no bail this time and I was remanded straight into custody to await my upcoming case at Leeds Crown Court. The police even gave me a parting 'goodwill gesture' by deciding to waive the possible charge of theft concerning the 'gentleman's coat. They were content that I would be off the streets for a reasonable period of time. Little did I know, I was about to begin the most harsh term that I would ever spend in any institution and it would test my endurance to the maximum.

CHAPTER 16

I decided, whilst I was again on remand at Thorpe Arch Remand Centre in Wetherby, to plead guilty to my robbery-with-violence charge at Leeds Crown Court. What would be the point in contesting it? The victim knew me and had already placed his hand on my shoulder at the identity parade. It would seem wiser to throw myself at the mercy of the judge who would be expected to show me a little leniency due to my early plea and saving the cost of a trial. This would be my very first time at not contesting a case but I was in a very tight corner with no means of escape. I was to be sentenced to two years imprisonment from the most feared judge on the circuit in the day. A certain Judge Pickles. Whilst we prisoners were detained in the 'bridewell' below the court and inquiring as to which judge would be presiding that day, the name Pickles would be the last name that any of us would wish to hear.

All things considered I had come out of it very lightly although it grieved me that I had got my sentence for a robbery that gained me such a paltry amount of money. It did not even seem to register with me that my sentence was for the violence element of my crime and not the money because violence had just become second nature to me, and throughout this sentence it would worsen.

I had felt I had been let off rather lightly because out of a twenty-four month sentence I would normally expect to serve sixteen months as eight would be given back automatically provided my behaviour was good but, as always with me, this would prove to be a difficult target for me to achieve.

Here I was again in Armley Prison in Leeds and on the young prisoners' landing until I would be allocated a suitable prison to suit my needs. What most of us would do in any prison to get additional time out of our cells would be to request to be allowed to attend any of the various church services on a Sunday morning. Apart from the additional time out of the cell it would be possible to meet up with any of the prisoners that we knew that were in other wings within the prison, including the remand wing, as such meetings would not normally be permitted to happen.

Obviously prisoners on remand would be allowed many more luxuries than a convicted felon and there would be no shortage of tobacco on the wings of the remand prisoners. Unless any of us applied to see the doctor or other medical staff at the same time then the only other opportunity to come into contact would be under the roof and sanctuary of the prison chapel. It would be at these times that the sleight of hand manoeuvres went on that would put Paul Daniels or any magician to shame as the tobacco and drugs, the 'currency' of any jail, would pass hands throughout the service as we might be reciting the Lord's Prayer or singing hymns. I wouldn't have thought that our Lord and Creator would object to us gaining a little relief from the rigours of the prison life.

I had found myself in the very favourable position of, later, having Dick Frost on remand in the prison and Jackie would visit him and bring in extra luxuries for him to smuggle across to my wing. Dick had spoken highly of me to his adult friends inside the prison and that meant that sometimes the prison friends who had special permits to 'access-all-areas', because they had certain cleaning duties, would bring things over to me for a small reward of a few cigarettes or tea bags. It soon became clear to some of the younger prisoners on my landing that I did not want for anything and I would look after anyone who seemed to be struggling.

It was during this sentence that I met two very good friends from Leeds and all throughout this book I have not named any individuals because I do not wish to create any problem should they now have a decent life and wish to forget their past. However, I am still kept informed of the well-being of my two friends and know they would have no objection to being named and so, Eddie Cawley from Harehills and Steve Best, I shall always remember you both fondly as we played the system.

The usual procedure for young prisoners was to be sent across to Strangeways or Walton in Liverpool but I did not like the idea of being sent, yet again, to be in the company of the 'high flyers' as I called them. Fortunately for me my birth mother had begun writing to me and making regular contact, and so the Principal Officer decided that I should be sent to Swinfen Hall in Lichfield, Staffordshire, to afford me the possibility of family visits as Nuneaton, where my mother lived, was in close proximity to Lichfield, being only about twenty miles away.

By now Dick had been sentenced to fifteen months' imprisonment and been given a cleaning job, which enabled him to go from wing to wing, and he paid me a surprise visit to wish me well for the future and brought a plastic mug containing vodka with him to toast my departure. It may seem hard to believe until I point out to you that, in many prisons, the warders are the ones that are responsible for bringing in a lot of illicit contraband, and sell to the inmates at an extortionate price. Dick had done just this and paid over the odds to have a bottle of vodka brought in. The only 'clause' in the 'contract' is that the warder puts the spirit in a mug or cup and the empty bottle leaves the prison with him, and then it is never discovered within the prison.

I was informed that the very next transfer of adult prisoners going to Winson Green in Birmingham would also have me on board to take me to the Midlands, and so within a week I was at Swinfen Hall. Although it sounded like a stately mansion it held some of the longest serving young prisoners from all around the country, and I would prove to be serving one of the shortest sentences there. I would estimate that the prison held perhaps 500 prisoners and although it was classed as a high security prison with loads of razor-tipped wire surrounding the walls, there was all-in-all a very relaxed atmosphere, and it made a welcome change for me to have a single cell and enjoy the privacy that that offered.

The intended visits from my mother did not materialise, even though I was within twenty miles of her home, and I could only blame myself as I had sent quite a few abusive letters, and I suppose it had set the tone for my behaviour.

I was selective about who I befriended in the prison because a good percentage of these long-term prisoners were rapists and murderers. It came to my attention that one inmate in particular was a notorious offender against children and I could not understand why he had not been dealt with before by some of the others. I would not be so tolerant of this individual, as I have mentioned earlier, since their sort need to be taught a lesson. After logging his movements over a period of time I knew that he showered at a certain time on most days. I did not wait too long to put my plan into action as I absolutely detested the smugness of this low-life who had comfortably settled into his surroundings. I double-checked that the warders where in the office having their customary chin-wag, and then I made my way to our communal kettle and proceeded to mix the boiling water with sugar before creeping stealthily to the shower area, and looking through the window, I could see that my intended target was inside, whistling away merrily to himself. I caught him totally by surprise as I threw the contents of the kettle all over his neck and facial area.

I was gone by the time he let out his first scream and safely back in my cell and appearing to be reading a book, should I be asked what I had been doing in the time that had led up to the recent event. I would tell no one what I had done because I had done it for my own satisfaction, and perhaps all the parents, even though it would be highly unlikely that they would ever hear of the incident. If you ask if I lost any sleep over the matter, then I can safely assure you that I slept like a log. I think the warders had their suspicions that I might be responsible, but whatever investigations took place soon petered out and the matter was soon to be forgotten.

On most evenings we would be allowed to play football in a very large main yard and we had a very good football team which played in all of the local leagues. Some of the other teams in the league would perhaps play on rough-shod council grounds or park football pitches, but for obvious reasons we would never get the chance to see these as we would be required to play all our games 'at home'. I think the other teams preferred coming to play on our pitch, because it would be tantamount to playing on turf like Wembley Stadium due to the constant attention the pitch would receive, and on each match day it was always in pristine condition.

I was put to work in the Concrete Shop where we would have a giant mixer on the go all of the time and we would put concrete into different-shaped trays along with reinforcing wire and place metal pins through the holes provided. When the concrete had set we would tap the pins out gently and empty the trays, to leave us with the end product which we would then stack out in the yard.

I had already discussed with a prisoner I trusted about the possibility of an escape attempt as I had spotted a few little lapses in security. It would require us to loosen one of the bars at the window of the workshop toilet, which we did, and then replace it again, but this time with some weakened concrete. Each day on the wing we would steal as many items of clothing as we could possibly get and we knotted them altogether in a makeshift 'rope'. We then wound reinforcing wire around it and finally fix a grappling hook made from wire to complete the task. We hid the 'rope' within the confines of the workshop and bided our time until the ideal opportunity presented itself to us.

The work routine would always be the same. We would be permitted to leave the workshop to stack the blocks in the yard waiting for collection and, should the weather be cold, then donkey jackets were on hand to be worn out in the yard. The instructors in the workshop were not warders, but civilians, who came in each day to give us the tuition we needed to achieve the task. The only warder in the vicinity would be the one with his dog patrolling up and down the perimeter fence.

When break times came around we would be gathered into the workshop and a head count would take place. Once the roll call had tallied as it should, the main doors would be secured and the instructor would give the patrolling warder the thumbs-up to signal that all was well. The very instant that we saw the warder ease off from his duties as he believed his job was done, we scrambled to the toilet and removed the loosened bar and almost fought each other to get through the inviting gap. We found ourselves out in the yard and with the assistance of a welcome blind-spot we hurled the 'rope' up the wall until it made contact with the coils of razor wire. To avoid any lacerations we spread a few of the donkey jackets across the wire.

We were not to know the layout of the area outside the prison wall and, as in this case in all the best laid plans, we would not be aware that there was an army camp alongside the prison and the area was to be quickly surrounded, which led to our immediate recapture.

For the first few days afterwards I would laugh and smile to myself at the furore our escapade had caused, but the smiles would quickly disappear with the reality setting in that I had just been sentenced to fifty-six days in solitary confinement by a visiting Magistrates Court. Most misdemeanours in any prison are dealt with internally, but if the matter is of a more serious nature, then visiting Magistrates need to be called in. They would soon be sent for again!

Instead of the customary four books normally allowed from the prison library I would now only be allowed two, so the choice became easy to select the thickest books in there to maybe provide me with adequate literature for the week. I found myself reading all of the Russian classics; Tolstoy, Dostoevsky and Pushkin, which surprisingly, made good and time-consuming reading. The warders in solitary make no effort whatsoever to converse with anyone, and it would be days at a time before I even heard any voice.

When I came off my solitary exercise period one of the warders accused me of loitering and pushed me rather heavily against the wall, causing bruising to my face and I accused him of assault. As it was a serious incident the visiting magistrates would be called to deal with the case, and after very little or no deliberation, they came to the conclusion that I had made a false and malicious accusation and for this I was to be given an additional fifty-six days in solitary confinement and, as was the case before, I was to forfeit fifty-six days remission. So in the space of just a few weeks I had landed myself with an extra four months in prison and the same period in solitary.

I was unhappy at the way I had been treated and took the decision to go on a hunger strike to draw attention to my plight, but this proved to be a futile exercise that would get me nowhere. In any hunger strike scenario the system allows an individual to go three days without any undue concern, but once that period had lapsed they are duty-bound to monitor that person on the prison hospital wing. At each meal time a meal would be placed in my cell and remain there until the next meal was then brought in to replace it. The hunger pains became unbearable as I paced the cell, trying not to even look in the direction of the food. I lasted until the fifth day before common sense prevailed and I realised that my actions would gain me nothing from my tormentors and I completely demolished my next meal like a ravenous wolf.

I had a little relief on only the one occasion when in solitary, when a fellow prisoner, who worked in the gardens party and was responsible for maintaining the football pitches and surrounding lawns, threw a tiny parcel into my cell, which contain a handful of 'magic mushrooms'. The hallucinations were incredible and when my cell door was opened for me to empty my chamber pot I drifted aimlessly out onto the landing, giggling hysterically with no sense of direction until the warder took me by the arm and guided me back behind the door. I imagined him laughing that night with some of his colleagues whilst he informed them that I had finally lost the plot and gone stir crazy when, in reality, I had just had my craziest, happiest night in a prison ever! It turned out that the mushrooms were growing in abundance on all the grassy areas around all of the football pitches.

I was coming to the end of my four-month stay in the punishment block, but it then transpired that the governor had other ideas, and he informed me that, due to the malicious accusations I had made against one of his warders, he was fearful that that some of the warder's colleagues might seek retribution, so he was not prepared to release me back into regular circulation and for that reason I would remain in solitary, supposedly, for my own protection.

I would now be allowed to smoke again should I choose and I could also have my radio and other personal things back, but I would remain secluded from the other inmates. I buried myself in educational books and absorbed knowledge like a sponge, but I was also very confrontational with the warders as I was very aggrieved at the governor's decision.

On the odd occasion a warder would open my cell door and push me against the wall whilst challenging me to a 'one-to-one' and insisting that, should I get the better of him, it wouldn't leave the four walls. He would twist his hand tightly into my abdomen and give me a little punch on my chin.

To the warders who might be reading this who worked in that punishment block at that time, could I just say that your behaviour was not very commendable and how you could have looked your partners in the eye at the end of your shift is beyond me. You were the biggest bullies I have ever come across in my whole life. I was a young boy, just twenty years old, and I don't know how you could live with yourselves.

Once it became clear to me that the governor was not about to have a change of heart anytime soon I petitioned the Home Office, requesting my case be reviewed regarding my confinement in the punishment block, but the matter was soon to be taken out of their hands as I reached adulthood and became twenty-one years old on the 9th December, 1974. Their problem was solved for them, and without a word of warning I was to be 'ghosted' to the adult prison where I had originally come from. I could no longer be held in a young offender's prison.

I was not exactly given the 'key-of-the-door' upon reaching the milestone of twenty-one years as was customary in England at that time, but I would be out of solitary, or so I thought!

Because I was regarded as an escapee I would have an escort comprising of two warders sat either side of me in the back of a taxi that would take me back to Yorkshire, my native homeland. I would be handcuffed to both of them. The journey passed without incident and never had I been as happy to see the castle on the hill that was Armley Prison in Leeds. However, my joy was to be short-lived!

CHAPTER 17

I was an adult now, but if I thought I would be treated like one I was sadly mistaken.

After completing the formalities of the paperwork and the official handover I was informed by the warder on reception that my reputation preceded me, and I was regarded as a 'hot potato' who would soon be leaving this prison, but meanwhile, I was to be placed down in solitary until the decision had been reached as to my destination. Leeds, like many inner city prisons, was simply a dispersal jail and in next to no time most prisoners would be sent to various locations, thereby creating the cell space for the constant influx of new detainees.

I was told within a few days that I would be transferred to Ribbleton Lane in Preston but that I would need to go via the next transfer to Strangeways and then proceed the short hop to Preston when it was possible. On arrival at Strangeways the governor greeted me by saying that I had already attempted to escape from one prison, and he was going to make sure that I did not do so from his, and announced that I would be placed on a 'Category A' list. I argued that I had not been allocated to his prison and should be permitted to travel onwards to Preston, but he said he had now taken the decision to overrule that and I would be serving out my sentence as a 'Category A' prisoner in his beloved Strangeways.

I was given, along with others, what can only be described as a Court Jester's outfit. All the way down one leg was a long yellow stripe of material, and on the opposite side of my jacket ran the same yellow stripe, thus implying that you were a coward who tries to run away in their opinion. All of us who were on the escapees list were to be accompanied everywhere we went by a warder who carried a book which must be signed with the time I had left my cell, where I had been, and the time I was placed back in my cell. It is yet another form of punishment, albeit with the bonus of me having a single cell. I would be required to take my clothes off each night and place them in a box outside my cell and a night light would be left on all through the night. This was so that the 'night watchman' would be able to check every fifteen minutes that nothing untoward was taking place.

Review boards would sit each month and make a decision as to whether anyone was a low or high risk absconder. If anyone had decamped from an open prison, which was quite a few, they would find themselves sooner rather than later back amongst the normal regime, but in cases such as mine less consideration was given and I was to have a long and continued spell with these restrictions.

It may seem a big plus to be placed at the front of every queue but that is not the case. The end result was that I found myself back in my cell almost as soon as I had come out of it. Whether it be visiting the library, the doctor's bay or the canteen, we would get the same treatment. First in, first out, and then escorted back to our cells. Other prisoners would be ushered well back to prevent any contact with us, and on completion of our tasks or duties we would be whisked away and normal service would resume for all the other inmates.

It was on one of these occasions I was to rub shoulders with the infamous Frankie Fraser who had been a major player in the Richardson torture gang of London. I now know a great deal more about how Frankie had been constantly mistreated and brutalised at that time, and most prisons would only be prepared to accept him for six months at a time and he would be expected to be moved, sometimes at night, at the drop of a hat. Frankie Fraser took more beatings than I could ever have imagined, and on meeting him at the time, the man had a manner about him that I admired as a young boy. As I have grown older that admiration has been replaced by total respect for a man who never bowed to the system. God bless you Frankie for surviving all they put you through, and it will always remain a lasting pleasure for me ever having had the slightest contact with you.

All of us escapees were interned in cells on the second landing, thus making the night warder's job to observe our movements during the night at regular intervals a little easier. We were scattered about on all of the five different wings and we would be constantly moved from cell to cell and from wing to wing to curtail all of the imaginary escapes that in a paranoid way they believed we had planned. Movements would be restricted on a daily basis but I would soon become acclimatised to the rigours of the regime. At least I could strip off in my cell and have a full body wash, whereas the rest of the prison would have three prisoners to a cell, therefore making it difficult to carry out the same procedure. Of course I always have the discomfort of any voyeuristic warder watching at my spy hole but I learned to disregard all of this.

The only time we would be allowed to mingle with other prisoners was during our exercise times, but we would miss out on the full hour because we were brought out later than the others and shouted to come in earlier. Even then we would only be allowed out if extra warders were available to oversee the exercise yard.

I had lost so much of my remission for good behaviour on this sentence that I had not even bothered asking or attempting to work out when my actual discharge date was but, by chance one day, I saw in on some official document, and to my astonishment it was to be on the 24th December. Considering I had not celebrated a Christmas on the outside world in the previous five years, it gave me a target to aim for.

Strangeways could be a brutal jail and some of the warders did not try to conceal the fact that they were 'Nationalists'. In actual fact some of them openly displayed National Front emblems on the lapels of their uniforms and I pitied some of the abuse any of the immigrants would have to endure at the hands of these people, but that's not to say that other prisoners were let off any lighter. This was a regime were I would be more than happy to stay under the radar and spend the majority of my sentence behind my cell door, thereby avoiding the limelight and ensuring no situation could arise that may jeopardise my festive release date. As I had done before, I did a lot of reading and studying.

For anyone wishing to further their education, strange as it may sound, there is no better place than a penal establishment. There is access to the best education imaginable by way of Open University degree courses and the like. If anyone was to try to study in the outside world there are the added distractions of social evenings out or celebratory occasions but, within a prison, once that cell door closes, no one is going to knock the door and interrupt you and the time is completely your own. I was beginning to educate myself far more than any of my childhood schools had ever done and I had gained a reputation of being a very learned man. Some of the other inmates would loan me books detailing the suppression in America, and from being slightly racist in my formative years, I then began to change in a very big way.

I would read Stokely Carmichael, Malcolm X, Angela Davis, and the injustices of people such as the Soledad brothers and I had a great sense of disbelief that these sorts of incidents could take place in a country they would proudly call 'the land of the free'.

I regretted many of the things I had done when I was in my younger years and much of this literature had opened my eyes. Or was it simply due to the fact that I was beginning to grow up a little now I had reached adulthood? I had a lot to reflect back on considering I had just reach the tender age of twenty-one and already had been to a detention centre, approved school, borstal twice and three different prisons. I mean, don't get me wrong, I knew I was not likely to end up being a Catholic priest but nor did I aspire to be so 'institutionalised' as I seemed to be. I was not a bad individual. I had just been dealt a harsh hand in life, but I also sensed that the time was ripe to correct my behaviour. Overnight I had become very politically aware and a much more balanced person and although this one sentence had taken an eternity to complete I promised myself that I would attempt to retain all of this new positive attitude ready for my imminent release.

In the prison system of today one could find oneself still waiting in the reception area all through the morning waiting to be discharged, but on this occasion I would find myself going through the main gate bright and early, and at the same time as the warders were coming through to begin their shifts.

The sentence had certainly been an endurance test and

challenged my resolve to the extreme, but that would quickly be forgotten as I walked the streets of Manchester. It mattered little to me that there was an absence of snow. It was Christmas. The Festive Season. And more importantly I was out of prison to celebrate. Rather belatedly I had been given 'the key of the door' to mark my coming of age!

CHAPTER 18

I had always been a full-on conversationalist but I had spent so much time in solitude that a few of my friends, who had taken the time to meet me at the train station, were concerned for my sanity as I no longer conversed as freely as I once did. I had lost the art of conversation. A lot had changed whilst I had been away and the streets were alive, with drugs being readily available everywhere, and I for one would not be complaining. I would get back to designer fashion at a later date, but for now I was more than content to be seen in patched-up jeans, cheesecloth shirt, clogs and smelling of petunia oil. Although a possibility of a return to prison was on the cards due to my ever-increasing involvement in the drug trade, I chose to ignore my fears and became more embroiled in what appeared to be easy money. At the time I had no money or prospects of a job once I was released, and if I wanted to be able to consume drugs at the same rate that everyone else was, then that consumption would need to be financed from somewhere.

I became a very laid-back individual and I would be constantly 'stoned' due to one substance or another. At times when I couldn't afford to buy narcotics in any great amount I would experiment with items on sale that had a label informing anyone that the contents should not be taken internally. I would go into any pharmacy and upon reading those words on a product, it was as if it was a direct challenge to my tolerance and I would, rather foolishly, dilute any of these medications until it reached a stage where it could be drunk. I am not prepared to name one particular substance which my friends and I would knock back in the day, as it resulted in the death of a very close friend and I would be the one who discovered the body. We would purchase this substance from the chemists, dilute it and then drink it down and the hallucinations made our eyesight so out of focus that, before we took it a second time, we went to the second-hand shops and purchased a pair of strong spectacles with 'jam-jar lenses' just to align our vision a little.

On this fateful occasion I awoke in a heap on the living room floor and went to rouse my friend who seemed asleep on the settee. It quickly became clear that he was very cold and had passed away. I knew that other people were asleep in the upper rooms and therefore I knew that he would very soon be found. So, rather selfishly, I left the property. I have relived this moment over and over throughout my life and I could not change the situation, and it seemed it would serve no purpose staying around to answer awkward questions from the police as the other occupants would need to do.

He was my very close friend and he had always taken drugs, long before I met him, but his parents were not aware of this and I suppose needed someone to blame and I fitted the bill. I felt an emptiness with him not being around and obviously I felt duty-bound to attend his funeral.

In hindsight maybe I should not have done that as his mother, in full view of the congregation, attacked me and raked my face with her nails, and I was totally embarrassed and left the church very shame-faced. The coroner had returned a verdict of death by misadventure and that's exactly what it was. It could have happened to any one of us. Miss you always mate!!! We were silly kids and up for just about anything and I would give anything to be able to turn the clock back.

It certainly made me reconsider the rashness of my actions and I no longer took part in non-established experimentation, although, in other areas of drug abuse, I began to spiral out of control for a while in an attempt to black out the tragedy. I had become a very bedraggled figure and my hair resembled a member of the rock group, Led Zeppelin, and I looked and acted more like a hippy every day. But for all my appearance I would still seem to be a person with an amiable nature, but my violent past and unpredictable behaviour would command a lot of respect too.

It was around this time that everyone around the whole country seemed to be taking LSD tablets, and I was introduced to people who needed an outlet in our area, and I had been put forward as a man who could be trusted. These LSD trips were far and away better than the 'false pretenders' of today and I would have some enjoyable evenings not being able to comprehend what was taking place for hours on end. I look back fondly on that period as we had a lot of fun, and the people who manufactured the tablets had a sense of humour themselves. They produced strip after strip of red, white and blue tablets to commemorate the Royal Jubilee. It only came to an end when police, working under cover, infiltrated the gang who had produced millions of tablets in a remote farmhouse in Wales. It became famous worldwide and was given the code name Operation Julie.

I would trade thousands of these tablets and build up a regular custom for them which proved to be very profitable indeed. One hundred tablets could be purchased for as little as thirty pounds, which could then be sold individually for between one and two pounds depending on whether the customer was a close friend or not. But, either way, the mark-up would be a good one. I tried to take hardly any drugs throughout my business dealings because I would need a clear head if I was to stay one step ahead of the police. Dealing in this particular drug and in the amounts I was trading would almost certainly lead to a lengthy prison sentence, and I had not been out too long, so it was a prospect I did not relish.

It would not be right and proper for me to name any of my cohorts during this period but we all know who we were, don't we lads? And you could do no more than agree that we ran a very tight ship and enjoyed our profits. Unfortunately for the manufacturers it all went wrong and they would get extremely lengthy and harsh sentences and our days of making hay would come to an end prematurely.

Police estimated later that taking out this one factory led to there being ninety per cent less LSD on the streets of the United Kingdom and it sent the street price from one pound up to five pounds because of the shortage on the street. I still managed to get some tablets for a short while from some of the members of the Satans Slaves Hells Angels Chapter in Bradford, but eventually even that source dried up.

I had made some good contacts along the way and now the drug of choice seemed to be amphetamine sulphate or 'speed' as it was more commonly known. I had come out of my shell a little more since I had come out of prison, but I was still somewhat reserved in my manner. However, all of that was about to change with the introduction of this 'helter-skelter-type' drug which would allow me to go for days without sleep and give me an increased awareness like no other. The clientele would be rather different, and many attended music festivals, so I would also travel to these on regular occasions to sell my wares. My sense of adventure had returned and along with it, the art of holding together long conversations, and in actual fact I would swivel my head around like an owl to ensure that everyone was listening to me whilst we were sat around the camp fire at the festival. I had lived the life of a monk whilst in solitary confinement all that time, almost as if I had taken a vow of silence but, after consuming 'speed' it would be impossible to contain me even for a moment. I would make a lot of new friends and also contacts for future drug deals while at these venues and it was sad to see the festival season come to a close until the following summer.

On looking in the mirror one morning I was surprised at my appearance, because although I had accumulated a reasonable amount of money, I felt I looked rather shabby and it was not an image I was comfortable with at all. If anything my image seemed to scream out that I was possibly a drug dealer, and so I made the decision to transform myself back to one of my previously smarter modes of fashion. The long tousled hair and the semblance of a goatee beard were the first things to go on the agenda, before I set about changing my wardrobe and with it my image and my whole persona. The transformation was instantaneous and I marvelled at the change along with the realisation that I would no longer stand out from the crowd and draw attention to myself.

It was around this time that I started to associate with some similarly smartly-clad lads who drank in a public house called the *Red Lion* in a small town called Heckmondwike that was close by to Dewsbury. I had not only managed to change my appearance but I had also managed to put distance between myself and Dewsbury, therefore doubly ensuring the means of avoiding the spotlight. All of these lads had formed a scooter club bearing the name of the pub and I shall remain firm friends with Phil Terry, Lee Cass, Vic Asquith, Tez Trepiak, John and Peter Schofield, and too many more to mention. Although Kev Hanson deserves a special mention as he was killed regrettably in a car crash in Amsterdam. All of these lads were my family for many years, and we still maintain strong bonds to this day and ties that can never be broken.

The Red Lion Scooter Club was to become renowned throughout the country amongst other scooter clubs, as we visited every coastal area in the United Kingdom. All scooter clubs would have their own means of identification, a sort of trademark, and ours was in the form of the obligatory crash helmets all painted lime green. The helmets would distinguish us from other clubs and are still worn today as the legacy has been passed down to the present day members who still 'fly the flag' for the club to this day.

In our day we would travel to seaside resorts on bank holiday weekends and meet up with other suchlike scooter clubs from just about every city and town imaginable. Our club was made up of a very fearsome sort of motley crew and each and every one of us was very heavily tattooed with mainly homemade offerings. To do this we would dismantle an alarm clock and use the mechanism to make our very own tattooing gun. There would be a bank of needles tied by cotton to the alarm 'trigger' and we would wind the alarm pointer round until it hit the spot that set off the reaction. The needles would, by this time, have ink running down from the cotton, having previously been dipped into the ink. Off we would go doing a very basic job for a short spell until the alarm needed rewinding again. Many a home in those days would have one parent or other tearing their hair out trying to fathom out just where their alarm clock had gone, as they needed it to help them get up for work the next morning. Little did they know that the clock was being utilised by us for a more leisurely pastime.

Our club would be feared at any local meetings within Yorkshire but we also had a certain notoriety that spread far and wide and we were afraid of no one. When we reached our destination our arrival would be greeted with a lot of respect but also with much caution, because we could be a very unpredictable bunch and were famous for enjoying the odd fracas. On scooter runs in our day there were no longer the 'Rockers' as rivals as in the older days of Mods and Rockers. We 'Mods' would have to create our own friction and have the occasional melee.

I was rumoured the rock group The Who were planning on making a film all about the long-standing mod culture, and a few years down the line some of our own club's members would find themselves playing major parts in this movie. They would find themselves down at Brighton filming for weeks on end and, due to the rugged appearances of some of our lads they would be riding in the film on scooters accompanied by Sting, the founder member of rock group The Police. The private joke amongst us was the knowledge that String himself struggled to master the art of even starting his scooter up, let alone riding it!

The film was to be called *Quadrophenia* and to this day has stood the test of time as a masterpiece in British film-making and I never tire of watching my scooter friends making the vital contribution that they did.

Generation after generation have kept this way of life to the fore, and I could never envisage much to change that. In actual fact my own younger brothers would also, at a later date, form their own scooter club bearing the name of The 3 Aces, and as was the case with other clubs, they would decorate their crash helmets in a distinctive way. In the case of my brother's club they wore a white helmet with a strip of blue fur over the middle resembling a Mohican hairstyle which made them easily recognisable. In later years we would form an alliance and meet up on many coastal runs.

Days seemed to be happy indeed with my band of brothers, but, as always in my life, things were never to run smoothly and if I believed my days of spending time in prison were over I had been sadly mistaken. One of my friends in the club had taken pity on me as I recounted some events of recent years and he took it upon himself to recommend me to his employer in the hope that I could turn my life around, and I was duly accepted as a member of the team in a rag-baling warehouse. For a short while I enjoyed the fruits of my labour but the old 'work hard – play hard' ethos always got the better of me and on a weekend I would constantly be found fighting outside pubs or clubs.

It was after one of those skirmishes that I found myself under arrest for a brutal assault outside one of my familiar haunts, and I was bailed to appear at Dewsbury Magistrates on a date to be announced at a later stage.

The timing of this incident could not have been worse as I had just met a girl called Julie, who would later be the mother of my first born child, David, and for the first time I recall I seemed to have a little stability in my life. Julie came from a respectable background and I am sure people would have advised her of the folly of getting together with a 'wild card' such as myself, but obviously she had taken no heed. The assault had taken place before I had met Julie and I would need to explain my pending court appearance at an appropriate time, but I was not in a hurry to do so for fear that I would lose her affection.

The dating game would be an expensive game at the best of times and I felt the need to impress, but it would not do my tight budget very many favours and, not for the first time, I began to question my wage structure and I encouraged my fellow workers to down tools and let me attempt to negotiate a pay increase. There would be no union representative as such in this sort of warehouse and the manager refused steadfastly to even give any consideration to a raise and, if we did not get back to work immediately, he said he would call the police to remove us from the premises. I assured the workers that we would be able to call his bluff and he would fulfil our demands but the end result was that we all found ourselves on the dole the following morning and signing on at the Labour Exchange!

My co-workers seemed in a state of shock as they pondered how to inform their partners that, in the short space of time since they had left that morning to go to work, they were now unemployed. My task would be doubly difficult because I had yet to even inform Julie of my impending court case. However, we would all of us be outdone by the fact that Julie herself had her own information that she wished to relay to me. She was pregnant and carrying my son, David!!!

CHAPTER 19

It seemed my life would always be destined to have drama in it, but how bad could the timing be on this particular occasion? Julie came from a very respectable family, and her family could have quite easily have encouraged her to turn her back on me, but thankfully they chose not to do so. Her parents had separated, but not before they had given birth to four daughters, all of them bearing the initial 'J' comprising of Julie, Jenny, Janet and Jill, and each of them were well-mannered and well brought-up girls. I am sure that, given the choice, their selection of a partner for any of their daughters would not have even remotely resembled me. I was every parent's nightmare I suppose, but instead of just tolerating me, they fully accepted me into the fold. Julie had the unenviable task of introducing me with all of my unsightly tattooed glory, and I cannot imagine the task was made any easier by the added news that she was pregnant with my child. Without this information concerning the arrival of their first grandchild I presume my presence would have received a much more cordial welcome, but it was more a case of perhaps an enforced acceptance.

At the time I was living in a squat, in a small area named Shaw Cross which was close to Leeds, along with four others and we had very recently caused a furore in the newspapers with the headline 'DEWSBURY SQUATTERS IN TOMB DRAMA'.

The local council had given us the option to vacate the premises as the whole block was due to be demolished on account of the antiquated state of disrepair that all the buildings were in. Being homeless, we took the decision to stand our ground and remain where we had settled for the past few months, and after barricading the downstairs section by the front door we went to the upstairs bedroom window to conduct any negotiations with the council officials. By this time the police had also let their presence be known and waited in the wings in the hope that they could arrest us yet again on any infringement of the law that enabled them to become involved.

Fortunately we were aware that the police could not actually get too involved in the situation, as this was a civil matter, and we set about taunting them incessantly, knowing that their hands were tied although obviously not pursuing the matter too far and then giving them the chance to get involved in a legal capacity.

After the opening salvo with the council officials, after it became clear to them that we had no intention of leaving unless they assured us we would be provided with suitable accommodation, things took a turn for the worse as they threatened us with the complete blocking off of the premises while we were still in it. They had told us of the instability of the structure due to the rising damp and faulty electrics but we had already discovered that whilst we had been in occupation of the property.

On many a cold morning, upon waking, should any of us place a hand on certain walls whilst getting dressed the voltage shooting from the offending wall would make our hair stand on end better than Rod Stewart or David Bowie. We were aware of all the building's defects but the bottom line was that it was still preferable to living on the streets. Of course it was a death trap but that should have given an indication of the lengths people can be driven to in attempting to acquire social housing, but the council insisted that we did not meet their criteria for any help.

Our 'home' was one of a block of ten buildings and all of them stood empty except ours, and the very minute they had got us out they would begin demolishing the whole block. This cat and mouse game continued throughout the day until the council tried to call our bluff and began breeze-blocking in the downstairs windows, and assured us that if we did not vacate the premises they would do the same with the front door, thereby giving us no means of exit.

By now the local press had arrived and began taking photographs of the proceedings, and the decision was reached by the council to withdraw at that point. Our case would be taken up at a later stage by left-wing sympathisers who took it upon themselves to pull down the numerous breeze blocks that had been cemented into the windows and furthermore, at an even later stage, the council would themselves be prosecuted for denying us access to fresh air by sealing the windows. Although we were squatters it appeared that we still had some rights and the council had overstepped the mark this time.

A bigger problem was that due to the publicity of the case Julie's parents had yet another insight into the lifestyle of the recently introduced 'son-in-law' and it did not bode well for the future. I wanted to lock horns with the council and take the incident further but common sense prevailed and I decided, along with the others, to leave the squat.

Within the property it was possible to go from one attic room along the building and gain access to each and every other attic and we did exactly this. As we moved from loft to loft we gathered up as much of the lead flashings as we could muster to sell for scrap metal. We all had one big farewell party with the proceeds and then went our separate ways in the knowledge that we had competed with and come off best with the local powers that be. It has often been suggested to me down the years that I should have tried some form of electric shock treatment to try to curb my aggressive behaviour, but I can assure you that I received more volts through my body in that derelict house than all the council's annual Christmas lighting!!!

By now Julie and I had moved into a bedsit in Cleckheaton and in any normal set of circumstances it should have been a case of waiting for the happy event, but I had the small matter of an outstanding court case to contend with. My past always came back to haunt me, it seemed. It was not as if I could blame anyone but myself, but I just wished that my path in life could be blessed with a little more good fortune than had been the case so far.

It was not to be as I was sentenced to nine months' imprisonment, and although it was a small enough sentence to ensure I would be released in time for the birth of my son, I left the court with a heavy heart, with the image of Julie crying in the public gallery. Every time I had been sent to prison in the past it mattered little or not at all, but this would be a whole different set of circumstances and I had responsibilities to other people to take into account. I found myself in the all too familiar setting of Armley Prison in Leeds. When would this cycle end? I cursed myself and the situation. This needed to stop, but I had to come to terms with this last predicament.

In any prison I ever visited, it does not matter how long my absence had been, it soon became apparent that the same individuals were to be seen going round in the same circle of the exercise yard as they had done thousands of times before, and I had no intention of becoming a part of this exclusive club again. I was no company for anyone as I felt a deep sense of remorse for what I had done to Julie and her family at such an inappropriate time, and this would really now need to be a very big turning point in my life, hopefully.

As is always the case I was 'rubber-stamped' in next to no time and would be on the next available transfer to Strangeways in Manchester. Anyone who has been in this place will tell you it has always had a notoriety amongst prisoners of being one of the biggest cesspits of all our penal establishments, and thankfully this was about to be the last time I would set foot inside the place. I had time to have a fleeting glimpse of the now disused 'hanging tower' before I was whisked through the door into the reception area.

The next stage of the induction is that prisoners have to stand around a circular metal diamond whilst having constant instructions bellowed at them by whichever bully boy warders make up the welcoming committee of the day, and God forbid any poor soul who even lets one foot touch their precious diamond. The diamond stands in the centre of the big rotunda roof which was always Strangeways' prominent landmark until prisoners rioted and demolished it a few years later. It is a very intimidating atmosphere for any prisoner making his debut, but I had heard all of the shouting many times now and I felt no fear at all from these 'upstanding pillars of society' – the warders.

It definitely is not the setting to be in and have the cavalier attitude that I had, but on this occasion I was more than a little pissed off with myself that I was in attendance here. Usual procedure is the need to grab a bed pack of sheets and blankets, and then a warder allocates you a landing where you will live, and then gives you a cell number on that landing. I was unfortunate enough on this occasion to have grabbed a bed pack that had belonged to some previous 'leper'. When prisoners get discharged from a prison they dump their bed pack in reception and in more instances than not the next arrivals pick up the same packs and it's a continual cycle. Should the previous inmate not have particularly bothered with his own personal hygiene then the very next recipient would suffer the consequences. Within a few days therefore I had constant itching between my fingers and other joints and upon reporting to the visiting doctor I was diagnosed with impetigo, and if that wasn't a bad enough burden to bear, I was also informed that I had scabies.

I was teased mercilessly by my two fellow cellmates and the taunts quickly turned into the physical bullying that I was to endure for the next three weeks from a very large Geordie lad, until he left. On one occasion he simply sky-dived from his top bunk straight into my bed and brought the full force of his knee into my mouth, causing my lower lip to bleed profusely. He panicked for a short while and set about clearing the blood away, fearful that a warder would open the door, but once he realised I was not the type of person who would report him then the bullying quickly resumed as he and his 'cell mate' on the lower bunk showed no mercy.

Julie was aware of my violent past and I promised her faithfully that I would avoid any trouble to ensure I would be back home at the earliest discharge date that was available. So these two inmates made my stay, for those few weeks, a living hell and with their bullying at its height, on more than one occasion I wanted to pick up my metal tray and attack them sneakily whilst they ate their meals or were performing their toilet duties, but instead I would just let them take the occasional fruit or other foodstuff that I was given, without complaint.

My surname is quite an unusual one and not easily forgotten so, if you lads are reading this, I would just like to inform you both how lucky you are that I let the situation go on as long as I did and I still have the scar around my mouth area to remind me. People like you are in all walks of life and by now I hope you both have had a rude awakening and got your comeuppance. You will never know how close you came to getting hit with a metal tray while you slept. You had my need to be released and the imminent arrival of my son as your salvation.

For the first time during any of my sentences that I had served, I found myself in the unusual position of receiving regular visits by Julie, and never once was I let down, as her father, who became a very good friend of mine, would drive her to Manchester and then wait outside until the visit was complete.

I would like to add to all of you partners that have remained loyal and write letters and visit regularly throughout long or even shorter sentences, that you are all worthy of the utmost respect.

I would look a sad and sorry state on those visits with the bruises and scars I had amassed, but my resolve was strong and I would not succumb to any added pressure that would possibly jeopardise my anticipated release date. In times gone by I would have reacted differently as far as possibly being rewarded with time off for good behaviour, because it all seemed irrelevant and immaterial to me as I really did prefer to stick two fingers up to the system. Now though my whole outlook had changed with the expectation of becoming a father. It is no coincidence that in many cases a person can be a habitual criminal until such a time as they become a parent, and so this would be the case with me. In the not too distant future I would again lapse back into this incarcerated sphere but, for now, I was about to focus my energies on a particularly pleasant period in my life.

On one of the visits Julie informed me that her father had placed a deposit on a small terraced house for us in Cleckheaton and I practically skipped back to my cell, content that I was making giant strides and I was now on the property ladder, even though I felt a little inadequate that I had not been personally involved in the purchase. I vowed to repay the trust these people had in me at the earliest chance, because I needed to exhibit better qualities than I had hitherto displayed to the family, who by now between them, had practically furnished our home and provided everything that would be required for a new born baby.

Although I had spent much longer periods than this in custody, the small sentence I had received seemed to take an eternity to finish as each day seemed to stretch on forever. In the past, doing a sentence and having no contact with the outside world would make me indifferent to anyone or anything but, to serve out a sentence and read mail every week detailing the hardship that someone else is encountering, makes for a very realistic and deserved wake-up call. I kept my head down and bit my lip on occasion and managed to complete my sentence without any further incident, and I would be released shortly with months to spare before the birth of my son.

I had usually had to make whatever journey by myself upon getting discharged, but I now fully appreciate that warm glow a man can feel when the big gates open and, plainly visible, there are people dear to him and an accompanying car to take him home. I would waste no time in correcting my behaviour and within hours of arriving back at our home I was applying for every job opportunity imaginable. I was out. I was happy and I was definitely blessed to have so much support.

CHAPTER 20

This was 1978 and mortgages were quite cheap, and I discovered that Julie had turned a very modest 'one-up and one down' terraced house into a very comfortable home. In time to come it would be sold at a very tidy profit and we would move into a much bigger property with three bedrooms, giving a little consideration to the idea of maybe extending the family.

My main priority was to find gainful employment and I finally made a breakthrough and was offered an opening with a company called Osborne Steel Extrusions in Low Moor, Bradford, which I gratefully accepted. The company was aware of my criminal past and still decided to employ me after I had implored them to consider that I was about to become a father, and I told them I wanted my home to be a home of a respectable nature, and I had put my past behind me.

My son was born in June of that year and Julie was

readily in agreement that I should name him David, thereby ensuring that I had a child to carry my name. My intention would be that he should never follow my path in life and I would attempt to give him the best possible start in his, and encourage him to fulfil every aspiration that I myself had never managed to do.

My job was giving me a lot of satisfaction, and the job description would be classed as a Mobile Operative, meaning we could end up on a different apparatus every day of the week. I much preferred this way of working as it gave me a better understanding of the factory and a certain versatility that would stand me in good stead should any shedding of jobs be required by the management. Of the thirty-two jobs on site I had mastered twenty-six of them and became renowned amongst the personnel managers as a ready-made reserve if anyone failed to attend for that day's work. I was quick and eager to learn, and as I worked in different departments, it gave me the chance to also note that there seemed to be a lot of inequality in respect of the allocation of overtime, and although I mentioned this to the Shop Steward, that I felt a lot of it bordered on racism, I felt that my comment was greeted with a great deal of indifference.

The Shop Steward was an elderly gentleman who was very set in his ways and I later learned that each time we had an annual pay rise it was because the Managing Director and he would have enjoyed a 'drink together'. This information came to light when the elderly gentleman died and it was proposed by a majority on the shop floor that I was to be the ideal candidate to replace him. I was called up for my introductory meeting with the Managing Director and he assured me that he had always maintained good industrial relations with union representatives, and went as far to say that he would drink with them socially on the odd occasion. His faced paled to the same grey shade as his suit when I informed him that I was there to represent a body of men and in no way would I be prepared to fraternise with him in any shape or form. I have to admit that I instantly relished my position of power and enjoyed the hold that I appeared to have over certain members of the management sector who had previously been a little harsh towards me.

I was sat at the Managing Director's table and being greeted with a firm handshake and such enthusiasm that you would have thought that we were related by blood, whereas in reality the same man had walked past me on hundreds of occasions without the slightest acknowledgement. The hypocrisy that existed between white collar workers and the general workforce was staggering, and I would learn much more about the ways and means to manipulate my position to the benefit of us all.

For all that senior management held the positions that they did with their privileged silver spoon backgrounds, I wielded far more power and could bring the whole plant to a complete standstill with just a wave of my hand. The image I portrayed to the Managing Director would not be one he preferred, and on many occasions I sensed that he resented the fact that he even had to negotiate anything at all with me. This was confirmed when one of his personnel managers informed me that he had described me as a little 'toe rag' with little or no education. Hearing such comments rankled me and without letting him know that I was aware of his remarks, I set about taking the gloss off his previously unchallenged empire.

When I called my first overtime ban I made a slight blunder. The Managing Director, poking fun at me, informed me that due to me not having cleared my decision with the head office of the union first, it was therefore regarded as unconstitutional behaviour and he was well within his rights to refuse to negotiate with me. I was a new recruit to this game and he seemed to relish in the fact that he appeared to have me over a barrel, but I had honed my skills in the jungle of the prisons and I was not prepared to back down and give him the satisfaction of gaining even a minor victory. My members placed their trust in me wholeheartedly and when I called them together to inform them I would need to lift the overtime ban they seemed disappointed, until I told them that it was up to themselves, as individuals, if they had a darts match or were required to babysit the family children or any other excuse they could possibly dream up. The ban had been lifted but it would still prove to be ineffective as my members supported me to a man and did not make themselves available. Touché! Checkmate!

I would lock horns with this man on many occasions and he quickly appreciated that I was far from the uneducated 'toe rag' he believed me to be. I would enjoy having him squirm in his seat, but I would much rather have been a fly on the wall at the times he sat with his superiors being berated about lost production. I could milk my position to the maximum and I often did. If I got to work after a particularly heavy weekend of partying and was not in the mood for any manual labour, or even if I had been given a task I did not like, I would merely invent a dispute of sorts.

In any dispute the usual procedure is to take up that problem with the immediate foreman, and if I deemed his response to be unsatisfactory I would go a stage further to the personnel manager, and ultimately all the way upstairs to the top man. This would be a time-consuming process which could take a whole day to complete, while all the time my machine would be switched off and I would find myself on just an 'average' bonus for the duration of the shift.

Come on you lot! Haven't any of you ever played the game? None of us ever got paid enough to sweat blood!

Another good ruse of mine would be to conceal completed work throughout the very large workshop floors and underbook the work I had finished, and then apply for weekend work. As in every company there would be shortage of white-collar workers on a weekend because they prefer the luxury of leisure time with their families. The big difference is they can afford to do so because they are on a higher fixed salary. Obviously I would still have the inconvenience of being on site on the Saturday and Sunday, albeit without any supervision, which I would take full advantage of by having a game of cards or even having a sleep in one of the many overhead cranes. I would be adequately covered for my work output as my quota for the weekend would already have been completed during the week.

I needed the hours and the money to cater for my family, and if management could not be bothered to be in attendance on weekends, then just as night follows day, why should I show any diligence? Yes, of course I manipulated the system, and I doubt many people could say they had not, or would not, do the same. Things began to take a turn for the worse in the steel industry and the introduction of the three-day week and large-scale redundancies were about to decimate our industry.

We were led to believe that our 'saviour' was likely to be a certain Ian McGregor, later known by us as the 'butcher' of the coal industry, who had been drafted in from America to rescue the steel industry, whereas the reality was that he had crossed the Atlantic to prune our services before moving on to the coalfields. Why it should be feasible to give a person from overseas a large amount of money to decimate any of our country's industries, which mean little or nothing to him, is totally beyond me. By the time this man had finished with the steelworkers, other unions and especially the National Union of Mineworkers would be more than aware who Mr. McGregor was and, in Arthur Scargill, the new president of the union, he would have a more determined adversary.

In the blink of an eye, from being solvent, I found myself working a three-day week until we finally ended up completely caught up in a national strike involving steel workers. I had spent all of the previous years reforming my character and yet, through no fault of my own, I once again found myself embroiled in criminal activity.

In the initial stages of the strike I would need to walk four miles to Bradford Town Hall to be given a pittance in strike pay and also receive a basic food parcel containing essential food and certainly nothing extravagant. I got the odd bit of casual work with an electrician I knew who paid me cash-in-hand, but the work was not very regular and eventually we ended up being in arrears with our mortgage.

I had been content with my position in life and everything seemed more than rosy in my garden but, overnight, I had been placed in an impossible position and I would need to provide for my family by whatever means were available. I did not reach the decision lightly but if there are hungry mouths to feed then food needs to be provided to quell that hunger. The government had already set out their new legislation and people on strike would not be permitted to apply for benefits, and in effect they would starve people back to work. The measures used would be magnified much more during the forthcoming miners' strike by the Tory government, and the North of England at this time would be a very harsh place to live in.

Handouts and charity are all very well and good but I was a proud man and needed to provide for my family in my own untoward manner. I did not get caught up in any activity that may have brought the force of the law down on me. Instead I preferred entering derelict properties and if a disused copper boiler was in there, then that would be a bonus, but even the whole of the copper electric wiring in the property would suffice, and I would burn off all of the plastic coating and then 'weigh-in' at the local scrap yard with the resulting wire. These were the days when even the drainpipes and guttering would be metal-based and I would be a regular sight pushing my wheelbarrow about with the contents of that day's labour.

I did not even class what I was doing as criminal as this situation had been forced upon me. What is a man to do? Could anyone say that given a similar set of circumstances they would not react in the exact same manner? My son, by now, had been growing very fast and had started his first school in Cleckheaton, and his needs would outweigh any conscience I may have had.

The crisis in the steel industry soon spiralled out of control and the situation had deteriorated to such an extent that large-scale redundancies were called for. I had always been in a safer place than other workers because of my status as the shop steward. I had always played the 'union card' when I chose to because even in any disciplinary matter it would be doubly difficult to dispose of a convenor for fear the incident could end up at a tribunal, and me possibly claiming constructive dismissal due to my union duties. But in my heart I just knew that the industry was dead on its feet and it would be tantamount to flogging a dead horse to expect some kind of miraculous recovery, and so I decided to put my name forward for voluntary redundancy. It would be an understatement to say that I was displeased with the initial monies offered, and so I informed senior management of this whilst declaring that I had required a specific amount of money for an intended project, and their figure did not match my needs, and I would much rather keep my job. I was instructed not to be hasty and to leave the matter with them and, needless to say, I left with a much more substantial agreement by way of an enhanced ex-gratia payment.

I had been a thorn in management's side for many a year and I could perhaps have named my price for them to dispense with my services, but we parted company on amicable terms. For once in my life it had certainly proved a little beneficial to be a troublemaker. I had not anticipated the job market would be as difficult as it proved to be to break into and, although the redundancy package had given us some much needed relief in our financial situation, it would not last forever and I was very quickly to take two strides back.

Julie would need to take on bar work at a few of the local public houses in the area and I would discover the effects of long-term unemployment. Our relationship began to go completely off the rails and I could not blame her one bit when she left as, by now, I had begun to take drugs once again.

Amphetamine sulphate was to become my drug of choice, and I would go for days and nights without any sleep at all, and my home would become renowned as a late night party house and would be constantly full with undesirable guests who would not have any consideration for those sleeping in my house or any of the neighbouring properties. It was not very long before I was a little out of control, and when I would finally go to sleep, after yet another three-day binge, I would remain in bed for a complete day at a time, and on reflection, I am surprised Julie did not leave, with our son, David, earlier than she did. She had been tolerant enough, I suppose, but finally had had enough of the situation and I was to find myself alone with my thoughts and the realisation that I had lost everything that was precious, which for the last nine years had given me the stability that I needed.

After continued attempts to reconcile all of our differences it soon became clear to me that getting back together again was not going to happen, and upon hearing that Julie had even found another partner it finally registered that I had reached my 'sell-by date' and I could blame no one but myself.

The parties continued and so too did the drug abuse,

albeit with the proviso that none of my fellow revellers should contact me on a weekend when I was allowed to have some precious time with my son. Eventually bouts of depression would descend upon me and I would go to some very dark places and I would feel unwanted and unloved, apart from my son, whose love was unconditional.

My birth mother had become aware of my plight and suggested that I move back to the Midlands and complete the family fold as my sister, Maureen, had now settled in the area and I was the last missing piece of the jigsaw regarding her very large brood of ten children. So after assurances from Julie that she would never deny me access to seeing David, at any time I requested, I took the decision to move south to Nuneaton. It would be a different adventure now in the present climate, as all of my siblings were grown up themselves and the bonding process would be much easier. Nuneaton, here I come!

CHAPTER 21

I arrived in the mid 1980s and was soon to discover that it was not exactly the 'land of milk and honey' but that situation would change within a few years. I was not particularly interested in finding a job because, after recent events, I was a little bit disillusioned with the job market and I intended to enjoy myself for a while considering the breakdown of my recent relationship.

In the early days I would commute back and forth to Yorkshire and I was given a sharp reminder each time of just how austere it had become with the Tory government policies of trying to break the miners' strike at all costs. My neighbours of old would be enduring the indignity of being forced into attending the many soup kitchens in the area, but as always, the Northern miners would stand against ending the strike to a man and resist the need to go back to work to the last.

I had heard numerous stories of the heavy-handed

approach of the Thames Valley police towards the miners, but I was to encounter it myself while driving back down the M1 Motorway towards the Midlands. I had never learnt to drive and would need to rely on one of my brothers or a friend to provide me with the regular lifts to see my son, as was the case on this occasion. The strike was in the later stages by now and a bitter division came about with the Nottinghamshire miners, who had voted to return to work with a breakaway union and 'flying pickets' would be headed for the area in their thousands to prevent their return to work.

As we approached Newark, which is close to Nottingham, we were flagged down by some very arrogant police officers, who demanded to know our destination. I attempted to explain that we were heading for Nuneaton, but upon hearing my Yorkshire accent one officer insisted we turned the car around and return in the opposite direction. I demanded that he checked the voting register in Nuneaton, thereby confirming that my family did actually live in that area, but he was adamant we were, in his opinion, flying pickets and he was not prepared to let us proceed. I challenged him again and insisted he had no right to prevent my freedom of movement in a free and democratic society such as our own. His response was to bring his baton down heavily across my upper thighs. It was obvious we would not be allowed to pass so we backtracked and had to choose an alternative route, but this left a bitter taste in my mouth.

I would come across the Thames Valley police many more times in later years when they would be responsible for 'crowd control'. Shame on all of them who brutalised working men and their families whilst waving large wads of money that they were paid in overtime, and the cowardly acts of excessive violence while they were in plain clothes bearing no insignia.

I was glad the North was behind me and for the first

time I was looking forward to blending in with my family and especially my brothers, who by now had gained themselves a fearsome reputation within Nuneaton and beyond.

The surname, Ginnelly, could be advantageous in some respects, but it also had its drawbacks, as within no time at all I found myself unable to get served in various public houses simply because of my surname. I was fortunate that although my younger brothers were well-known in the locality, and especially to the police, I was the 'new kid on the block' and the police in Nuneaton were unaware of my existence – I quickly set about turning this to my advantage. I still had many long-standing contacts in Leeds and other areas of the North and so I very quickly established regular deliveries of amphetamines to be dropped to me.

My name would have been mentioned in police whispers many times I would imagine, but it would be many years before I came to their attention by being arrested, so for the immediate time being I would remain under the radar and reap all of the rewards that went with that.

I had a succession of girlfriends but it just seemed I was incapable of settling down with anyone. Being apart from my son was like missing a rib, but I would never let him down at any time and if I did not have a lift I would use public transport to either take him home or bring him down to visit. Our bond could never be broken, but I readily admit that I put him before many a relationship during the early period of me breaking up with his mother, but I never regret doing so. On the odd occasion after I had return my son to his mother I would 'kill two birds with one stone' by making a visit to one of my drug sources and transport the wares back by myself. Until such a time came when the amounts of drugs increased to such as extent that I would feel unsafe travelling alone by train!

Although I had got into a regular pattern with my son he must have thought that on each visit that his dad was a 'gypsy' as I have lived in no less than thirty-seven different homes within Nuneaton. It was not like I was deliberately being evasive or anything, but my elusiveness would also be of benefit to me as no one knew where I lived from one minute to the next.

With regular criminal connections a matter of trust is absolutely standard, and to be expected, but the shady world of street-dealing with drugs puts oneself on a precipice and amongst people who would sell their soul if the need arose. Amongst any of these people I would chastise anyone who let slip my surname, because these reprobates are the very ones who have the loose lips that sink established ships. I was wearing the Captain's Cap at this time and I would not want my ship scuppered by some loose-lipped moron. My merchandise was of a greater purity than had previously been available in the area, and so I quickly gained a regular and very profitable clientele.

Apart from local custom I would be able to offload some of my powders, potions and pills at football jaunts or scooter runs to the coast, and within trusted circles, it would be known that I was the main man to see, if anyone needed a livener, as such, to combat any fatigue. If I was to keep going back to Leeds and other football grounds I would need to change my allegiance if I wanted to have breaks away, as I had always been a diehard Manchester United supporter, as the tattoos all over my hands will bear testimony to.

Patrick (Paddy) and all of my other brothers would follow Leeds United all around the country, and so it was with a heavy heart that I began to do the same and start to accompany my brothers and friends to many grounds of lower-league teams that I had not visited before. My tattoos caused one or two skirmishes in the early days amongst some Leeds supporters who resented the fact that I now followed their beloved team, but I soon became a familiar figure at the games and would be accepted as a 'convert'. No one could even question my acceptance as the endorsement had come from some of the 'hierarchy' with the 'Service Crew' which was a notorious section of the Leeds supporters and had been given the seal of approval from the top. If I had once thought that Manchester United fans travelling away from home could be a formidable force then Leeds were simply in a league of their own and feared no one. We would travel up to Leeds regularly on most match days and although the journey could soon be covered in a half-decent car, we would never ever seem to be in the ground by the time the game kicked off and we were noted for our tardiness, which became a topic of fun.

All of my family have strong connections with likeable rogues from up north and many a link-up has been conducted while in attendance at the football matches, and the same applies to the links forged during scooter runs. Needing to drive many miles along A-roads would be very time consuming and tiring and the arrangement would be, that should a bank holiday's destination be a southern coastal area such as Brighton, Yarmouth or Southend, then the northern lads from the Red Lion Scooter Club would break their journey up by staying in Nuneaton as guests of the Three Aces members on the Friday night. The alternative should the run be to a northerly area such as Scarborough, Morecombe or Southport, then the Three Aces members would have the Friday stop-over in Heckmondwike.

All of these friendships can never be broken, and to the present time have lasted for three decades or more and long may they continue. Obviously the villainy side of it has petered out a little, but in those days there would be no better way to do business than from county to county, thereby decreasing the likelihood of being arrested. We would always be travelling on one Motorway or another and CCTV would be limited back in this time, and the cover of a scooter run or a football match contributed to many profitable 'ram raids'!

Nobody can be held to account now and I would not be prepared to disclose names, but cars and scooters would be stolen from both areas and given new identities and then transferred from county to county and the same would apply to the movement of stolen credit cards and counterfeit money. Villainy seemed to be the way of the world and I had not had the misfortune to have been arrested again for many years, so why should I have the need to care about my actions? I was carefree and enjoying living the life. My brothers and I had become a very tight-knit unit, and at times, when any one of us would not be 'earning' it usually worked out that one or more of the others would have funds available and we would be endowed with a very hectic social schedule and be in the pubs and clubs on a regular basis.

These activities had their setbacks as I had found to my cost in the past, but for the time being I was certainly not of the opinion that 'crime doesn't pay'. I was moving kilos of amphetamines at a time and I was making thousands of pounds on some deals. I would have drugs secreted in various hiding places around the town and would keep all of the locations in my head, and I would guess that even to this day there may be a parcel still hidden that I had forgotten and overlooked. I do not want you all to be rushing for your metal detectors though, as the parcels would contain vast amounts of powder-based substances concealed in Tupperware cups to prevent leaving any fingerprint identification.

I would have a close friend who would hire a car in Nottingham, where he lived, and come to pick me up under the cover of darkness. We would then go to the

Northern Soul all-nighters throughout the country, as these venues would be packed full of prospective customers. I would not be stupid enough to take large amounts with me to the clubs, preferring instead to make the initial contact, take the order, and arrange to meet in some secluded area during the week. Obviously we would carry our own personal supply to consume for our enjoyment, and that would be hidden in the wing mirror of the car.

Should we ever be unfortunate enough to have a routine 'stop and search' by the police we would observe them practically tear the car apart and watch their bemused faces and the scratching of their heads as they waved us on would be a joy to behold. We would not need telling twice to go on our way, and even though our eyes would resemble flying saucers because of how drugged-up we were, the police would not be able to explain it as the supply would be so well hidden. We would laugh hysterically for mile after mile as we drove off into the distance.

I would arrange to meet 'customers' from as far afield as Luton, Hemel Hempstead, Derby or Wakefield during the week, and it had reached the stage where I could not spend the money quickly enough as the notes piled up. For anyone thinking it seems a glamorous lifestyle I can assure you it is far from it, as each and every day is spent on one motorway or another and the hours spent 'working' far exceeds a regular 40hr week that respectable people have to contend with.

Added to that I had recently met a girl called Marion and we had begun to build a home together. My long absences would cause many arguments between us, and I could fully understand her fears for the future. I would be away for long periods and stay in expensive hotels in London and bring her gifts back from Harrods or other exotic stores – it would be scant compensation for my repeated absences but I was making a lot of money and it was difficult to stop.

By now Marion was pregnant with my son, Kyle, and he was born in June of the year 1987 and he would be quickly followed by Troy in June of the following year. What was it with June? All of my three sons would be born in that month!!

With the birth of Kyle I should have once again resumed my share of the responsibilities of fatherhood, but as always I was too busy being 'Jack-the-Lad' and still enjoying the single life as such, even though I should have focused on building the family nest. I was still attending football matches and even enjoying the odd scuffle, which I should really have grown out of, but anyone who knows will confirm that it is like a drug of its own.

In 1988 our team, Leeds United, for a change had shown a consistency throughout the football season that had not been seen for many a year. This culminated in an F.A. Cup semi-final appearance against Coventry City at Hillsborough Stadium in Sheffield.

With money being no object we acquired lots of tickets for ourselves and many of our friends from Leeds, albeit for the section of the ground that would hold Coventry supporters. On the day of the match we explained our dilemma to the South Yorkshire police, who would be more than happy to let us join our own supporters in the Leppings Lane end of the ground, thereby ensuring segregation from the Coventry lot and hopefully causing less trouble.

It was the year before the ill-fated incident with the deaths of almost 100 Liverpool supporters. Even after all of these years I can safely say that I have never before or since been so packed into a crowd so tightly, and on many occasions throughout that afternoon I was fearful for my own safety, and I even dreaded going through the extra time that would have to be played eventually. I had never been so relieved to leave a football ground in my whole life.

All of us had set our hearts on an outing to Wembley Stadium for the final but it was not to be as we lost the match in extra time, and the journey home down the motorway seemed to take an eternity, especially so being surrounded by Coventry coaches and cars all making the same journey south.

I needed a break from football for a while, or at least attending the actual games. Non-league games would provide a satisfactory replacement and the policing at these games would leave a lot to be desired.

CHAPTER 22

I think Marion preferred it when I seemed to be spending much more time in and around Nuneaton, and although she expressed her concerns about me going to watch Nuneaton Borough, it was if she was resigned to the fact that boys will be boys.

I should have realised that I was placing myself in the limelight more and more but I had become complacent and perhaps a little too cocksure that I would forever escape justice. I would be literally given a rude awakening when my front door and back door were broken off their hinges in a dawn raid by about twenty drug squad officers. They were all over the flat like a swarm of locusts, and in and out of every nook and cranny searching for drugs or money.

It may be hard for anyone to appreciate but I can assure you that the large police presence is there to not only intimidate the occupants, but also to possibly do a much quicker sleight-of-hand than any magician as money or drugs that may be found do not always find their way back to the police station as evidence. In any police force the length and breadth of this country the one unit that can be more corrupt than any other is the drug squad, and the reason being that they come into contact with vast amounts of money and drugs and the temptation to pocket some of it becomes too much for them. Anyone not wishing to believe that widespread corruption exists between these particular officers is walking around with blinkers on.

The police in the 'dawn raid' would be sorely disappointed on this occasion because my 'golden rule' was never to have drugs in any amounts on my own property. I had learnt on an earlier occasion that I could gain access to the prepayment meter box on the television by using one of the keys for the window locks on the recently installed double-glazing windows. I had placed several thousand pounds in bundles of a thousand, secured by elastic bands, into the box and although they searched my home with a magnifying glass, they came up empty handed. I was in no way unnerved by the hustle and bustle and their loud-mouthed manner, and got myself dressed at my own leisurely pace once I had been informed that I was under arrest for intent to supply controlled drugs.

My two small children, Kyle and Troy, were still in nappies and cried continuously from their cot, and I demanded that they be taken to my mother's home which was in close proximity to our own home. They announced that the children would be accompanying both parents to the police station to ensure that other family members could not be notified of any police activity in the area in case further arrests were imminent. I was aware of the underhand methods that the drug squad officers employed, and it would still not encourage me to make any admissions or even comment. Their intention would be to place added pressure on the mother, who they regarded as the weak link. I would discover later that certain officers had teased my partner incessantly about the various sex toys they had come across in a bedroom drawer in our bedside cabinet. Heroes to a man, are these supposed upholders of law and order, but worse was to follow.

They informed me, during the taped interview, that from the allotments at the rear of my home and across the canal that they had monitored my movements for a few weeks and they had witnessed some drug deals taking place. I knew this would be difficult for them to do and I was tempted on a few occasions to respond, but as I had always done throughout my criminal career I replied on each occasion with the words "NO COMMENT."

It became apparent that I had been observed in a communal bin area at the end of the flats but the reality was it would have been impossible for them to have a clear sight of the enclosed area and I could have simply been in the bin area to dispose of rubbish. It was like a game of chess as they placed a Tupperware cup on the table and informed me that the substance found inside was now on its way to be analysed.

The cup would have had a sports sock wrapped around it tightly, and I was quite confident that no fingerprints could be found and, to be quite truthful, for that to be discovered in a communal area it could belong to any one of the fifty-plus residents.

I was given unconditional bail while the matter was investigated further and I would walk out of the station confident they would have a great deal of difficulty proving the charges.

I shut-up shop for a considerable period now I knew I had come to the attention of the 'Heavy Brigade' and it would make no sense to take any unnecessary chances. I would soon run out of money and I would need to subcontract out a little work to my brothers so at least I would have a little income finding its way to my pocket.

By now we had all begun to frequent a public house in the middle of the estate called the *Donnithorne Arms*, and to be truthful, it was the only way forward being as how my family would not be welcome in the pubs and clubs in the town centre. Our family had a violent and fearsome reputation and although many police forces throughout the country will try to deny that 'no-go areas' exist I would refute that very strongly. The joke amongst us was that perhaps the police should try a different approach and maybe arrive sitting on the roofs of their patrol cars because, on the few isolated times they had dared to intervene in any disturbance the cars had been tipped over and extensively damaged with the occupants still inside.

The 'Donni' became a stronghold, and a lawless premises with any number of top-of-the-range cars on the front car park and a meeting point for lots of likeable rogues from every corner of the country. It became our own little night club and taxis could be seen arriving at all times of the day and night. The area became our own version of the Bermuda Triangle because anyone entering the premises would not be seen for days at a time and it would continue in this vein for many years to come.

Games of cards would take place with the one rule of no credit over the table while a game was in progress although personal belongings could be used as collateral and a player's car keys could be observed amongst the stake money in the middle of the table on numerous occasions. The only disruption to any of the drinkers would be when the early morning cleaners arrived. Everyone would be herded into one room until the cleaning was completed and then everyone would later re-enter the cleaned room to resume their session. Our friends would make the journey down from Leeds on regular social visits because they were very impressed with the way that my family ran the whole show.

It was on one of these visits that the police decided to let their presence be known and having realised that the majority of us would have retired to our own homes after a hectic weekend they would conduct their early morning raids at nine different addresses on the estate simultaneously.

I had a friend staying with me from Leeds who I shall call 'Wak' and he knew my golden rule was never to have drugs in my home, and so the 'goods' he had purchased by the kilo he had left at another friend's house to be picked up by him at the time of his departure, which sadly for him, happened to coincide with the dawn raid.

Once again my home would prove to be empty which seemed to disappoint the police and it made me think that they did not feel confident about the first set of charges, and would have been more pleased if they had captured me in a 'live' situation to bolster their claims of my guilt in the first incident.

My friend 'Wak' from Leeds would return at a later date with his solicitor to claim responsibility for the two kilos of hashish he claimed he had hidden at the other property without the tenant's knowledge. It was a nice gesture of him to do so but it would leave him serving a two-year sentence later on. But not before he had fled the country and had one last mad jaunt around Europe. He will resurface later in the book.

It would not be long before I answered my bail on my own charges, but for the time being the police seemed to have come to the end of their tether and wanted us behind bars at all costs. My brother Patrick and I would be isolated from the other detainees and ferried over to Rugby police station while everyone else was under lock and key in Nuneaton. I suppose the police hoped against hope that if they gave the illusion that me and Paddy were already on remand in Winson Green Prison that it would encourage the others to loosen their lips. Our friends were made of a lot sterner stuff than that and no incriminating information would be forthcoming from our trusted circle. Out of the twelve people arrested only two would be facing charges and how they must have cursed themselves for jumping the gun.

Because a lot of Leeds associates had landed in the area the police had presumed that a lot of 'trade' must be going on but they had misread the situation and had ended up with egg on their faces and someone needed to pay the price. That someone would be me!

I answered my bail and was informed I was to be charged with intent to supply Class A, B and C drugs. To this day I have no reason to lie and the contents of the plastic cup were for my own consumption and consisted of several bags of amphetamines, each weighing seven grams, eight trips of LSD, and finally a small amount of lonimin, an amphetamine-based prescription drug. The whole case rested solely on what two officers claimed they had observed me doing and so I decided to plead not guilty and contest the case.

Let me first state that I am an individual who will throw his hands up and accept the situation if I have been caught in a 'fair cop' but what was about to take place with the officers' testimony was a complete fabrication and a tissue of lies. Three days were set aside for a trial at Warwick Crown Court and as in all cases on the first day the plea bargaining comes into play, and it is possible to get a reduced sentence if any savings can be made by not incurring the costs of a lengthy trial.

Barristers confer with each other and I was told that if I pleaded guilty to the possession of the drugs then they would be happy to waive the intent to supply charge which carried a heavier sentence. I refused and insisted I wished to contest all of the charges thinking I had a reasonable chance of walking out of the court a free man.

My confidence would take a knock when I had the opportunity to look the jurors in the eyes. I glanced from one to the other and quickly came to the conclusion most of the jurors appeared to represent middle-class suburbia, and would never think it possible that a police officer in the witness box could even begin to not be telling 'the truth, the whole truth and nothing but the truth'. I smiled at an older type lady on the panel and received a frosty response and I had an image of her riding a bicycle with a basket on the front when she was pruning her roses. I was quickly sensing I was a condemned man and I went through the motions of protesting my innocence rather half-heartedly.

On the second day of the trial the jury were brought by coach to view all of the vantage points that the officers claimed to have been in while they watched me in the bin areas and this should have been my strongest point of contest, but the jury may as well have been knitting all the way there and all the way back for all the amount of interest they showed. They retired to consider the so-called 'evidence' on the third day and within a few hours returned a verdict of guilty. There had been no customers or witnesses to assist the police. There had been no fingerprints to determine my guilt. The case rested on the two upstanding officers' evidence and the jury chose to believe all of their 'evidence' and there I stood awaiting my fate.

The judge rambled on a lot in his summing up and every criminal worth his salt will tell you his speech goes over one's head and the only time I paid attention was to listen to the tariff. *Did he just say three years? Have I just been sentenced to THREE YEARS?* The sentence was excessive but I would have to take into account that I had challenged the court and I had incurred additional costs. It can be an unfair system but it's the risk every man who is on trial takes. Had I taken the offer put to me on the first day of the trial before proceedings had begun I would have been given twelve months' imprisonment but I had taken the gamble and lost.

Did he just say three years? That was all I could think while I heard Marion's tears and the screaming coming from the public gallery. My mother was also in attendance at the court and I ushered them both out of my cell, below the court room, while I gathered my thoughts. *Did that bastard just give me three years?* I had not been in a prison for more than a decade and I would need to acclimatise to my new situation.

I had done the tour of duty in Northern prisons and I would now need to take in my stride and introduce myself to Midlands jails. Winson Green was my first port of call and although a dirty prison it seemed a little less regimented than other inner-city jails. While I was down at the canteen's hot plate getting my meal to take back for myself I was greeted by some lads from Nuneaton who worked in the kitchens and told me it was long, hard work but it had many perks and they could swing it with their boss and get me down there working.

I did not need to even think twice because not only did the job seem satisfactory but I would also be in the company of inmates that I knew, and I was soon in the living quarters of the kitchen workers. We would still be in cells on the lower landing but because we handled food we would be allowed a shower and change of clothes daily, whereas the rest of the prison population would need to suffice with one shower per week.

The kitchen in a prison is a very large place and the need to cater for fifteen hundred inmates three times daily can be a very demanding job. We would need to rise an hour earlier than the rest of the prison to prepare breakfasts and five hundred eggs would be boiled in each of the three large vats. It is a hive of activity and upon cessation of duties at the end of the day we would fall into our beds exhausted. To keep up our energy we would have an enhanced diet and our wages would be substantially more than the other inmates. The biggest 'bonus' to accept would be that we had less time to reflect on our misfortunes because we were kept so busy. It makes much more sense to be kept busy as opposed to lying on a bed, in a cell, dwelling on such things as problems at home.

One of my friends from Nuneaton was a trustee in the kitchen and therefore had a key to access the stores and weigh out the day's requirements for the kitchen. It was nothing to him to purloin the odd bag of sugar and the occasional box of yeast, and with a few tins of pineapple, we would leave the whole mixture to ferment until we had a pineapple hooch that would be like paint stripper on the linings of our stomach but, let's face it – a drink is a drink. I think the warders knew, but just turned a blind eye because we worked hard and I suppose they felt we deserved a little fun.

I enjoyed life in the kitchen, plus the fact if I stayed in Birmingham it would be easier for visits, but Birmingham was the same as Leeds. It was a dispersal prison and within four months I discovered I was being transferred to a Category B prison in nearby Wolverhampton.

Featherstone Prison housed some of the most monstrous prisoners I would ever encounter in all of my years inside and I was expected to mix freely with inmates who had had sex with a few dead bodies, and another who had raped his own mother.

I did not know even one inmate in here, whereas if I had been interned in Yorkshire I would probably come across a few prisoners from my past. I would not be aware of anyone's criminal history and so, whilst engaging in conversation with the librarian inmate, it was pointed out to me that he had slept with bodies at the morgue where he had previously worked. In any prison it comes in useful to befriend inmates who work in the libraries because they can order books you may wish to read, but this person sent a shiver down my spine.

Each evening when my cell door would be opened for socialising I would kick it straight back shut as I did not wish to mix with these sorts of offenders. I was advised that if I did not make the effort to integrate then it could be detrimental to my consideration for parole. I did not really care. As far as I was concerned it would be best for all parties concerned if the decision was taken to transfer me back to a mainstream prison.

I became a recluse and put my name down for educational courses rather than venture out into the workshops where most of the prison population would be. I studied Advanced English and also completed a Royal School of Arts Degree in communication skills, and I buried myself in education to help pass the days, weeks and months away. I threw myself into my studies and it would help to cover me for the periods I would remain in my cell by way of explaining that I was completing my coursework. I was in a very relaxed prison and would have had the freedom to walk about anywhere in the prison unaccompanied, but instead, I lived the life of a prisoner who had restrictions. That would be my choice and my way of dealing with this place.

Because I was sentenced for drug offences I would have more random cell searches than most, and whilst I was observing how thorough the searches could be I also noted the odd place where they did not pay too much attention. I would smuggle hashish in at times on visits by swallowing a lump wrapped in cling film and then the following day when I did my toilet duties I would need to squeeze my faeces into toilet paper until I made contact with the solid lump. Not a very pleasant task at all but the benefits far outweigh the indignity of the task at hand. I had noted that my school pens did not arouse much attention in the cell searches and so I would break the lump of hashish down into small pieces and then wedge them all tight up into the pen tops. As and when I fancied a joint I would simply stamp on the pen top and crush the case until I reached my goal.

This establishment more than any other honed my language skills almost to perfection, and the tutors, who came into the prison from outside, did a more than adequate job of schooling us – I thank you for the education you gave me.

Marion never let me down on any visit, even though by now she was getting a hard time from her parents and her support at the time contributed greatly to my completing the sentence with no disciplinary procedures of any sort. I had actually been in this prison without having a spell in the punishment cells, and surely that had to be an improvement for me. For that reason the Parole Board seemed to agree and I was granted an early release.

Had I been rehabilitated? That was a question open to debate, but I would soon be free to see what the world had to offer. I had missed my two little boys and it had broken my heart to be missing seeing them grow up, but I would soon make up for that missed time with them.

It was 1990, and I was thankful to be out and I would not have missed this period for the world. The fashion and drugs that were about to surface would change the world forever. I was itching to get involved in a few parties after the lengthy period I had just spent locked up, but the parties of this time and this particular period would be immense and remembered fondly by me forever.

It was ecstasy, acid, whistles and strobes. The Rave Culture had arrived. 1990 would be the summer of love!!!

CHAPTER 23

Shortly before I was to be released a few of our local bikers from Warwickshire had been transferred from Long Larton Prison in Leicestershire to complete the ten-year sentences they had been given many years before, for offences of manslaughter and affray with a rival gang of Hells Angels. This rivalry continued for many years and will continue to do so because a splinter group known as The Outlaws live by their own code of conduct.

I got on quite well with one of them whose name was 'Tick', who ended up in the cell opposite me and he had informed me of the stories he had heard of some new designer drug called 'ecstasy'.

Many bridges have been built with The Outlaws down the years and although at one time it would have seemed unimaginable that scooterists like us could possibly get on amicably with bikers, that was not the case within our circles. One of the 'Outlaws' clubhouses was situated within Nuneaton, and very heavily reinforced with a lot of steel shutters on the windows and doors of the property, and my family and I would conduct many a satisfactory business transaction there.

I am sure it would have confused our local police just how strong our bonds with each other had become considering the rivalry that existed between both factions previously. Obviously the police would have preferred everyone to be at each other's throats because whenever we formed an alliance it would be doubly difficult to try to investigate our activities, but unite we did and the bonds formed will never be broken.

I would not have to wait too long for the chance to sample and confirm 'Tick's tales of this wonder drug called ecstasy.

I had promised Marion faithfully that I would correct my behaviour upon my release, but as is the case with many felons, it could prove to be an empty promise and simply 'jail talk'. Every promise can be sincerely meant at the time but the reality is that once those prison doors are opened after a long incarceration and everything becomes accessible again, it is just too easy to fall back into an all too familiar pattern and this time it would be no different.

I did try, and had all of the best intentions in the world until the night I was introduced to my first little ecstasy tablet, which I was told had the tag name 'M25' 'cos you seemed to be on it forever! I kid you not! This was the holy grail of the drug world and nothing before or since has matched the euphoric state that these pills created. M25s would soon be followed by Doves, New Yorkers, China Whites and Dennis-the-Menaces and although the cost at £20 a tablet seemed excessive, it was a pleasure to pay it.

I had never experienced this sort of sensation with any drug I had taken previously and it had apparently arrived from the club culture in New York, but I would not have cared if it had arrived courtesy of Outer Mongolia. It was here, who cares how it had arrived? It created an empathy with everyone and such excitement had never existed before and a whole generation threw their arms around each other and partied like nothing else mattered.

I had made the effort and applied for a few jobs, but if I was to be truthful, I did not wish for any of them to lead to anything. After discussions with a friend of mine who lived in Atherstone, a village nearby, I struck a deal to purchase 100 ecstasy tablets at a cost of £8 each because of the bulk purchase. The 'Black Market' in drugs is no different to any large supermarket chain and sometimes deals and special offers are there to be had if the amount and the price is right.

It becomes a way of life and although it is not to everyone's taste it very soon becomes one's place of work and earns a living in the exact same way as would be the benefit of someone turning up at a factory to do a day's work. You may think that it seems strange that I had just completed a prison sentence and yet here I was right back in the same setting, but circumstances sometimes dictate that there appears to be no alternative. Marion had also taken a liking to this latest drug cult and it would have been virtually impossible to finance our consumption of the drug without some sort of finance of our own to sustain it.

My brother Paddy had by now opened a clothes shop in the town called 'Innovation' because the scene also required its own branded clothing and music, which went hand-in-hand with our lifestyles at the time. Most of us favoured the exclusive Gio Goi clothing range at the time, and it is still an ongoing fashion now and a very well-established brand.

The lifestyle in this period went completely ballistic, very much a 'white knuckle ride' for us all, but I can honestly say there could never again be a period to match it. We would pay the odd security guard, whose job it would be to patrol the industrial estates, a good sum of money to allow us access to one of the empty units on the estate to enable us to put on our own 'warehouse party', but obviously not informing the guards of that small fact. We would assure them it would only be a small gathering to celebrate a friend's birthday or some other celebratory excuse and after handing over perhaps two hundred pounds we would be given the green light to proceed but only on the proviso that we would collect and dispose of any rubbish when the 'party' ended. If any of you have ever attended a similar mad, full-on rave of that period you would know as well as me that the possibility of anyone on the following morning ever attempting to tidy up would be the last thing on the agenda. Who really cared? It wasn't as if that venue could ever be used again. There would always be other security guards happy to boost their meagre wages by way of the windfall that we offered.

Upon gaining access to any of these units the day would be taken up by people inside creating a backdrop of psychedelic colours and also electricians to make sure that everything would run smoothly. Alcohol would be sold at exorbitant prices from a hastily arranged bar area and local doormen who were close friends of ours would be employed as security men.

The police would always show up eventually but more often than not by that time a thousand people or more would be in attendance and the party would be in full swing. As these parties became more frequent it became a game of Cat and Mouse with the police who were constantly trying to locate our next venue before we could establish the base and make all the necessary phone calls. We were aware that some of our contacts had gone 'undercover' and turned informants, and we would know the ones as they were being a bit too inquisitive and we would give these individuals a lot of misinformation and red herrings to chase. We would send this group off on a wild goose chase and by the time they realised their mistake our party would once again be lifting the rafters.

The police numbers would soon be on the increase because the 'powers that be' must have concluded that the raves needed nipping in the bud, as more manic warehouse parties began to spring up everywhere and an alternative society was developing. Our 'alliance' with the Outlaws proved beneficial because we could then have our own private little gatherings in their clubhouse that they owned, and the police would prefer not to visit with regard to any complaints about noise because they knew they would be greeted with a hostile response.

It transpired that the bikers owned some property in North Wales as well as a disused quarry in that area, so the decision was taken to 'de-camp' a good section of the population of Nuneaton to North Wales. The police in Wales had been informed of our imminent arrival and, although the land was legally owned by our 'Outlaw friends', they still tried to prevent us from reaching the quarry. Helicopters circled above us for hours but all the spotlights could pick up was all of us running across the fields or scaling down the quarry face. All of us had abandoned our cars so to be quite truthful the police could have had twice as many road blocks and it would have made little difference. We had arrived! We were all 'pilled-up' and we could hear the music in the distance and we made towards the music automatically, just as a moth would be attracted to a light bulb. That night proved to be a total waste of police resources. Did they really believe that having driven all that way from Nuneaton in the Midlands that we would simply turn around at the sight of the first police blockade?

We would have many enjoyable full-on parties with our friends, the 'Outlaws', and I wish to thank them all for some very memorable nights and in particular my close friend, Pete, who is now President of the whole Warwickshire Chapter who I have a great deal of respect for and we will remain life-long friends.

Some of the 'Outlaws' have a fearsome reputation and many years later seven of their members would receive one hundred and ninety-one years in total imprisonment between them for the murder of another Hell's Angel. Gerry Tobin would be shot in the head on the M40 Motorway as he rode his bike home from a meeting of bikers.

Two of the men sentenced were from the Nuneaton area and would attend the club house at the time of our rave parties, and I can honestly say that I have never even had as much as an argument with any one of them. My friend Pete was recently voted in as President and I hope he will preside for many years to come.

The time had come to attempt to put on bigger parties and my brother Paddy went a stage further and put one on in Spain. I suppose he felt everyone needed a holiday as such but why waste an opportunity and so with the holiday came a 'do'. There would be no escaping the rave scene at this time and it would be one continual party and the pills being smuggled in, if anything, were getting much stronger. A lot of us throughout this period would prefer to drink water rather than alcohol whenever we were under the influence of the pills, because in a certain few the ingredients could contain heroin, which could be a bad mix with alcohol.

I was bringing a little attention to myself and I was fearful of further imprisonment and so I took the decision to accept a job I had been offered doing some industrial cleaning in Daventry even though the wages were not likely to be life changing. To all intents and purposes, if the police decided to watch me I would appear to be earning an honest crust.

Thankfully the boss would never be on site as he employed us to do his contract work and he would occasionally turn up unannounced during our shift to check on our progress. He was a self-made millionaire who lived in his sixteenth-century cottage in Wolvey, a sleepy well-to-do village, and would often show up in his cricket whites fresh from a game on his local village green.

As always in my life, if he chose not to be in the vicinity to oversee our work, I would settle for an easy day's work rather than sweat blood, and especially if the boss was more concerned with his 'run-rate' at cricket.

I would get picked up by the works van at 5 a.m. to reach Daventry in good time for a six o'clock start, and I lost count of the times I got into that van fresh from a party and unable to even focus on what day it was!!

The job was starting to be a little bit of a bind, and I would be so exhausted that upon arrival at the plant I would make for the boiler house and lay on a pile of industrial wipes and cloths and go to sleep on my makeshift mattress, and my friend would come and wake me if ever the boss showed up on the job. I would gladly have given the job up because it was interfering with my social life, but I quickly changed my mind one day when an opportunity came about that I could not refuse.

It turned out there was a bit of a shortage in Daventry with most substances, and it brought home to me the realisation that I had a lot of captive customers here in the palm of my hand. I was like Doctor Death on the shop floor and trading in just about everything and clearing a thousand pounds in illicit goods every week, and my actual wages became pin money. I would also take into the factory fake perfumes, aftershaves and even alcohol that had been brought back from various runs across the channel. As soon as my immediate foreman knew that I was going to give him a small percentage he gave me the entire shift to myself to offload my goods and he got someone else to cover my duties.

Come on!!! At least be truthful!! It's the sort of job that you have all craved for at one time or another. I was on the payroll and yet I could go and have a catnap as and when I pleased and not have any work to do, so then I could even have the odd tipple out of the alcohol I was selling. Happy days indeed!!

I acquired an infection on the sole of one of my feet and on talking to some of the other lads it transpired that they had contracted similar rashes at other times in the past. I believed we were handling hazardous chemicals and filled a bottle to take to be analysed by the dermatologist at my local hospital. My boss found out that I had done this and it would not be much longer before I found myself without a job again.

The chemical proved to be harmless but it had cost me the job of a lifetime. I felt it needed doing at the time and no matter how comfortable I am in my own circumstances I will always champion the cause of the underdog even though, on this occasion, it cost me my job.

The 'Donni' pub by now had become a hotbed of vice and attracted a particular sort of clientele and I just blended back into doing doorstep trade and dealing with any cars that may pull into the car park. I had a small Staffordshire Bull Terrier and I would just loiter outside with the dog until someone pulled up asking for drugs, and once they had placed an order I would tell them to go into the pub and have a drink and I would get back to them shortly. I would play with the dog by throwing him a stick until the right opportunity offered itself and then, as I stooped, I would pick up a cigarette packet from out of the bushes outside the pub. I would then go and serve my customer with some of the contents and then, after they had gone, I would go through the same procedure with the stick and dog until I could return the packet to the bushes.

At this time the brewery had sent a succession of managers to run the pub but all of them would find it an impossible task, and it became a running joke that most of them never even managed to stay longer than a month. It was rumoured that one manager felt so intimidated that he actually threw himself down the cellar steps, thus breaking his leg, in order to get himself out of the pub and the contractual tenancy.

On one occasion two foot-patrol officers came in to arrest one of the drinkers because of some domestic situation with his partner. It was made clear to the officers, one of them a female, that their presence was not welcome and to vacate the area but the male officer, full of bravado, trying to show off to his female companion, drew his truncheon. Within seconds they both lay unconscious on the floor and I have no reason to lie but the only one who struck the female officer was a lady who was drinking in the pub at the time. However, it was reported in the national press that 'lager-louts', the in-word in the papers at the time, had swung her around by the hair. Could I say that I am all for the power of the press but only when matters are reported in a truthful manner.

The manager of the pub at the time rang the police station to inform them what had taken place and the pub was quickly surrounded by every available officer. We gathered on the doorstep with pool cues or any makeshift weapon that we could muster and the situation became a bit of a stand-off until the commanding officer ventured down the path and negotiated the safe return of his colleagues. No charges or even arrests came about because of this incident but it let us know that the manager of the pub could not be trusted and he had to go.

The next landlord to take over became a good friend of our family. His name is Mick Barnsley and he lasted longer than all the previous ten managers put together. Mick would amuse us by dressing up as a different character most weeks and it would come as no surprise to be served by a pirate one day or a priest the next. Of course he would have been aware of what we were getting up to but I suppose he chose to turn a 'blind eye' to it all. He was in charge of a growing concern and we would be bringing in lots of additional custom from other estates, and the tills would be ringing so everyone would be happy for different reasons. 'Our' pub was a stronghold for many years and whoever chose to run it was simply a figurehead, whether they chose to believe it or not.

My boys were growing up fast and I lived opposite the pub so that it would be quite easy to spend long periods at home until the 'rush hour' at the pub began. I would advise anyone to have two children very close together because they not only have a constant playmate but with the arguments and fights that can result in fisticuffs, they can teach each other how to fight far better than any boxing club.

My relationship with Marion was under a lot of strain and I would be the first to admit that, selfishly, I was spending far too much time in the pub and leading the life of a single man.

I had become involved in the football violence scene again, and it may displease many people but the bottom line is it is a challenge between rival groups and none of us would set out to intentionally involve innocent bystanders. Nuneaton Borough Club had been drawn away against Swansea in the F.A. Cup and even though we were a non-league side we always prided ourselves on the way we would analyse the opposition, and with this in mind we attended a Swansea mid-week game ahead of our later cup match. Swansea's visitors on this occasion were Burnley. We filled a car and travelled to Swansea to do our little reconnaissance and target the likely ambush spots that Swansea may have thought they had. We entered the ground and mingled with some of the Burnley supporters in the away end and told them of our intentions the following week but you could see the look of disbelief on their faces with the knowledge of our club's non-league status. Little did they know of our history.

The following week on the day of the cup game we had thirty 'Bedford' vans full of just our own lads from 'The Donni' and at the head of affairs was my brother Paddy driving his Cosworth, which would later have its windscreen broken but that would be the only minor victory the Swansea lads would register, as we just took the place over and anyone of note in this sort of activity will inform you that having one over on Swansea in their own back yard is a notable scalp. The game went to a replay and Nuneaton police had advised Swansea fan club not to travel to Nuneaton, and the advice was heeded, but we had already shown them what we were capable of, so we did not even care about their absence from the match.

I needed to avoid these events and to not get involved, but it is like a fever and very addictive, and we were about to take football hooliganism to a different level because we had decided to travel to Europe at every opportunity to watch our national team.

It would be a break from the hectic schedule of drug dealing at the pub but also we would have the chance to dispose of some counterfeit twenty pound notes, and also get some additional use of some stolen credit cards that had been 'worked to death' in this country. Travelling with England abroad can be a very daunting challenge because we have never ever been welcomed with open arms in any country and each foreign visit is a potential minefield. But, what the fuck? Who cared? We were 'The Donni crew' and we would be on the ferry shortly. EUROPE, ARE YOU READY???

CHAPTER 24

On one of our jaunts into Europe we headed for Rotterdam to watch England play against Holland in a World Cup qualifier. My brother Paddy had purchased two American camper vans and wherever we went on our mission we would travel in comfort and be able to turn the chairs all of the way round while we played cards and lightened the load by drinking our way through mountains of alcohol.

We would visit Amsterdam first to do what all red-blooded males do in that country and take in the sights and visit the tulip factories (not). After we had been suitably relieved we carried on with our journey to Rotterdam, arriving in good time for the game. The first drinking tavern we arrived at was completely awash with England fans, and as always, we had a very good turn out of supporters. It became very boisterous as we sang all of our patriotic songs and it was quite a carnival atmosphere as we sipped on our first drinks since arriving. A few

Dutch supporters had gathered at the street across and after a little bit of banter and some taunting one of them threw a green tennis ball across in our direction. My brother Stephen strode into the street to kick the ball back towards the rival supporters, only for there to be an almighty explosion, the result of which blew my brother's trainer off, tore a hole in his jeans, and inflicted deep shrapnel-type wounds in his leg.

We discovered that the homemade bomb contained nails filed down to sharp points and, of course, explosives. When we leave our shores it always seems standard procedure as to how the local police react and today would be no different than any other previous time. As soon as the smoke began to clear we would find our own group of supporters chased down the street by the Dutch Mounted Police and baton charged and rounded up and then placed in a pen underneath the ground. I had been in many countries on England football excursions and the outcome never varies. I have been water-cannoned and gassed with C.S. gas and, more often than not, simply for being in the wrong place at the wrong time.

In my opinion Dutch and German hooligans are just as extreme in their behaviour but never at any time do any of their visiting 'Nationals' receive a fraction of the ill-treatment that we encounter when we visit their countries.

It was as if the Dutch police were of the opinion that we had detonated the 'bomb' and now we had to suffer the consequences and we would have to remain in this pen for the next four hours. At least we had an opportunity to break our hoodoo of arriving late for a game being as how we were practically within one hundred yards of the stadium. A bigger problem would be explaining why we had tickets for the Dutch end of the ground in our possession.

We knew people who 'worked' in Holland and they had purchased the tickets for us a few weeks prior to the game, but we would have to focus on finding any police officer who seemed to be of a friendly disposition, and this we did. After I had explained to him that we did not want any trouble and preferred going into the England section he was quickly convinced that we could not possibly be hooligans if we wanted to avoid trouble. He opened the gate and, after only releasing the people who were in my company, he ushered us into the ground and told us to enjoy the game. We laughed hysterically as we resumed normal service and began taunting the Dutch.

The outcome of the game would be exactly the same as it had been many times before and as usual England would conspire to lose the game and with it the opportunity to play automatically in the next World Cup. We caught the ferry back rather dejectedly, but at least we had done a little 'business' while we were out there.

After we arrived back at 'The Donni' it soon became clear that my brother Stephen was having complications with his leg and he would need to attend the emergency department of the local George Eliot Hospital to have the shrapnel removed. The wound was no more than we expected when we went abroad to support the football but God forbid if the tennis ball 'bomb' had ever landed on a table full of beer glasses, as it could have blinded anyone in the vicinity. The English may have a bad reputation abroad but I can assure you that other national teams' supporters should be held to account too.

On the next outing our destination would be Norway and the game was on the Wednesday night and we set out from 'The Donni' after loading the camper vans with the customary boxes of lagers. It would seem comical for any Customs Officers noting that we seemed to be doing an alcohol run in the reverse direction as we would be carrying that much booze.

We left early on the Monday morning and crossed over on the ferry to Amsterdam on the first leg of our journey.

On the way over we 'found' a wallet on the floor of the casino and because none of the passengers in the immediate vicinity seemed to be unduly distressed the decision was quickly taken to put the fine array of credit cards to good use on our travels. On landing we sampled some of the drugs that were readily available, without fear of arrest, and enjoyed the sights.

To say Holland is as close to England as it is, all of us may as well be on another planet, the setting is so relaxed and I could easily live in this country forever. After becoming suitably refreshed we would take a drive to Utrecht. This is a university city, albeit with other added attractions along the canal with a succession of boats containing girls from every nation of the world. It was possible to drive along the side of the canal at a steady pace until one of the girls became the object of my desire, and then I would board the barge and state my requirements and agree a price. A few of the girls may have got into trouble the following day when they discovered the notes they had received in payment were valueless. But we had no scruples as we made our way towards Germany by road to complete our next leg of the journey.

From Germany we caught another ferry across to Gothenburg in Sweden where we would come to the attention of Swedish Customs. We were herded into some sort of shunting shed and told to bring all of our luggage off to be searched for anything illicit. They thought it strange that we had taken the route that we had to reach Norway especially as we still had a long drive through Sweden and Denmark before we reached our destination.

A lot of the lads had thrown the cannabis resin away at the first opportunity upon realising that we were about to have a thorough search but I would not choose to get rid of my chemical substances which I had hidden in my underwear. On trips such as this I would always take to wearing Y-front type underpants because of the secret little pocket at the bottom where it would be quite easy to nestle my goods safely to avoid detection. I would be conscious of the fact that our journey was still an outward one, and certainly not the time to be getting rid of drugs we may need. We were waved on our way by the officials who constantly giggled, pointing to all the tattoos we had between us, but who cared?? We had driven away with the most important drugs still being safely in our possession.

The drive through Denmark is a long and boring journey with mile after mile of desolate forest land, and apart from the occasional moose or elk straying in the road, we saw little of any interest. As I have stated previously our little group had a bad habit of arriving late at games in Leeds but this little outing would take our reputation to a different level.

We had travelled through four countries and set off two days before the game was due to commence and we had now finally arrived in Norway at HALF-TIME in the match. The English supporters had been playing up with the local riot police all day long and I think the police had finally had enough. As we tried to find a parking space the police surrounded us and baited us by banging on the vans with their batons and we took the decision to remain inside as we realised we were the stragglers of our supporters and we would get the backlash and suffer the consequences of whatever had taken place throughout the day.

We would eventually drive away from the ground and try to find a public house to quench our thirst, but most places had either chosen to lock up early or were in the process of boarding up broken windows from any earlier fracas. Not that we wanted to hang about for too long after the discovery that it cost three pounds for just a half of lager.

We had not had much joy on this trip but it was about to become a whole lot worse when we arrived back in

Sweden. Since the time they had allowed us to proceed the Swedish Customs had become aware that certain members of our party were known to be involved in large scale smuggling of cannabis resin, and they had been instructed to locate us at all costs. Meanwhile we enjoyed a good drink in the pleasant surroundings of Malmo and set about compensating ourselves for the fact that we had missed the game.

We arrived at Gothenburg for the return journey but were informed our passports would be confiscated until further notice. Ferry after ferry departed and we seemed to have been there for an eternity while they stripped our vans down to the bare bones. We demanded the British Consul be brought in to deal with the matter because we knew we were not guilty of any offence. Finally a decision was reached that we would be permitted to travel but only if we agreed to sail around the Hook of Holland and would not actually be allowed to set foot in Holland.

We finally boarded a ferry but we would incur additional costs because the only ferry we would be allowed on consisted of cabins and an all-night disco and we would need to sail direct to Harwich.

Did anyone really think that we would be foolish enough to be actually transporting drugs back ourselves?? It was the same old story and I felt we had been needlessly harassed. Oh! And lest I forget! It was the same old story with our England team too, as they lost yet again.

Things were getting bad back in our own country as the government were trying to implement a bill called the Criminal Justice Act whereby they could limit all of our gatherings for parties. It had all become too much and the authorities had found their solution, it seemed, but not before many of us took to the streets of London with a mass protest that would challenge the ruling. It had all become a little heavy by now and lots of illegal raves would be getting 'taxed' at gunpoint. The atmosphere around a lot of the gatherings had begun to be very menacing and lots of people would be robbed of drugs or money which made life difficult, especially as there could be no police involvement.

We had all had our good times out of it and although I still intended to sell ecstasy I had chosen to find a safer outlet than some tin-pot warehouse with its makeshift security.

Was it government sanctions or heavy handed gangsters? Who knows how it all came to an end, but we had all filled our boots when it was in full flow. We now needed to accept the heady days of the early nineties, with their summers of love, had come to an end.

By now our pub, 'The Donni' had been managed by so many different people that I suppose it was a thorn in the side of the brewery that owned it. Even the hardcore managers that had lasted longer than most would succumb eventually and one of my brothers decided it was time for the family to enter the pub trade.

Obviously the local police would contest anything to do with our family surname and so it would have been an impossible dream for any of us to put our name forward to the local Magistrates for getting a licence to run the premises. It would therefore require a good, well-respected friend of ours to apply for the licence without the police being aware or they would lodge very strong objections.

It did not exactly need publicising that the pub was under new management as it had always been know as our stronghold. We made a few amendments and had the decor done to our own satisfaction and we had a recording studio built into the side of the pub for our very own D.J.s to mix their own music and put it on open sale.

As a final touch we hoisted a scooter up onto the roof of the pub and bolted it down above the front door, and this would become part of the pub insignia and could be seen clearly from quite a distance away. It was like our very own Jolly Roger. We were modern day pirates and 'The Donni' was our flagship. I would still do trade from the pub but business would be a little slow as even the ecstasy tablets had become of a much poorer quality now and prices had dropped considerably. The pub wasn't being run as it should have been either. All of us had been accustomed to drug dealings and so running a regular business had never been on the agenda, and the bills went unpaid until it reached the stage where the brewery decided to stop delivering beer. The easy option was taken to order from another brewery.

The pub had been bought out by our favourite manager, Mick Barnsley, and he had rented the premises out to my brother and he never regretted his decision to do so, but one or two breweries did. We would drink around the clock and laugh knowing that we had no intention of paying for the beer because we already had another brewery signed up for the next delivery. Having a family pub can be a good thing but the bonus of not needing to pay for alcohol consumed is more than satisfactory.

Me being at the pub all the time did not do my relationship with Marion many favours, and looking back now, I should have always known I was on borrowed time but I carried on with my hectic social life regardless.

We would all need to be in attendance at the pub to maintain the strength in numbers because it had recently been attacked by a rival gang from Coventry who released C.S. gas on the premises and the Fire Brigade shut the pub down for the next forty-eight hours for safety reasons.

The camaraderie of the early nineties had long gone and it would not be too long now before firearms played a big part in anything to do with the drugs trade. The police had begun to set up established vantage points to keep tabs on the pub from a distance, but we knew of one flat opposite the pub that they were occupying and so that increased our caution.

One of our friends dropped his guard, unfortunately, when he was out of the area and was photographed in a 'live' situation by some docks in Hull and he had also been sighted, with the same person, across the water in Holland, on an earlier occasion. We knew there had been a lot of police activity lately but no one knew that Her Majesty's Customs and Excise had been in the picture until it was too late for our friend. The end result was that Steve Craythorne appeared, along with others, at Birmingham Crown Court and would be sentenced to ten years' imprisonment for the importation of three million pounds worth of cannabis resin. It had been calculated that several previous runs had taken place and on each occasion in excess of one hundred kilos were being smuggled into the country.

A full episode of 'Crimewatch' on the TV could have been produced just with the characters who regularly drank in 'The Donni'. I have spoken to each of them in turn and none of them have any objection to being named in this book, especially considering that the crimes, as such, stem from a time long gone.

Rafael Viola and his brother, Alphonse, who had both completed a twelve-year sentence for manslaughter in a gang fight in Coventry.

Kevin Houston, who would eventually feature in the 'Hard Bastards' series that Kate Kray produced for a TV programme.

James Fenton (Irish Jim), who would very soon be found slumped in his car having been shot in the back of the head in a gangland execution. No one would ever be found or charged with the murder and to this day it remains unsolved. God bless you Jim. May you rest in peace!

We had another friend who never uses his surname but many will know of him. His name is Pete and he ran his own security company for celebrities and the stars. One minute he would be protecting the boy band, Back Street Boys, and the next minute he could be found jogging around Hyde Park with Madonna which was featured in the DVD entitled 'In bed with Madonna'. Pete was the subject of a Roger Cook (an Investigative Journalist) exposé and was set up for an arms deal by his own driver and treachery does not get much lower than being set up by the man that sits alongside you each day. Pete managed to get out of that particular scrape and still runs a thriving security business that provides security for the 'Big Brother' house now on Channel 5 TV.

There would also be leading members of 'The Outlaws' Hells Angels group in attendance at the pub, and anyone walking into our pub for an innocent drink and not being aware of its history would soon make for the exit on looking around at some of the unsavoury clientele. There would very rarely be any internal trouble and on the few occasions that there was then a quiet word in the back room would usually suffice, but if the problem could not be resolved by 'smoking the peace pipe' then the people involved would be dispatched to the cellar to sort out their differences.

In that same cellar, on rare occasions, should any individual have been caught out skimming money or double dealing they would have to suffer the consequences of being placed in a chair and hopefully realising they must not do this again. At these times the jukebox would be turned up to the maximum to mask the screams coming from the cellar. Fortunately it did not happen too often and that may have been because everyone knew of the existence of 'The Chair'.

It may seem a bit extreme reading the above comments but the same situations exist in many towns around the country and this manner of serving justice is not just exclusive to our inner cities. Where there are large amounts of drugs or money it goes hand-in-hand that violence will not be too far away.

CHAPTER 25

It had all become a little bit too much for me and I decided to retreat to the comfort of the family home. We had recently been rehoused to a three-bedroomed property in Tulliver Road and the timing could not have been more opportune as Marion discovered she was pregnant with our daughter, Demi, who would be the best Christmas present of 1995 for both of us. I had been quite squeamish at other births and had always taken the decision not to go into the theatre, but for some reason I just wanted to be there for this birth. I would not wish to exchange that memory for anything as I squeezed Marion's hand while we waited to be introduced to the most beautiful baby girl, and it proved to be the most exquisite vision I could ever expect to witness. Nothing could ever come close to that moment as I held Demi in my arms.

I had been given three sons and I think a man's mindset is totally different when a precious, delicate little girl comes on the scene. With all boys it's usually a straightforward case of teaching them how to play football or even climb trees or other boy-like activities, and although you love all of your kids equally there just seems to be a need to wrap a little girl in cotton wool. It changed my whole manner and outlook on life and I withdrew from all of the shady business and stayed away from the pub for long periods.

'The Donni' had just been renamed 'The Hanson Arms' after a close friend of mine had died in a car chase with the police in Amsterdam and a Yorkshire-themed crest with a white rose was created to commemorate Kev Hanson who had been a proper good grafter his whole life and was a very special lad who will always have a special place in my heart. One of my other friends who was in the car with Kev was Shaun O'Connel, who spent the next year in a wheelchair and has never fully recovered. I suppose these are sad occasions when crime does not pay but it's the risks we take and none of us would change it if incidents like this did not take place. I concentrated on my family life for a while and stayed out of the pub and drug scene.

I would take my two boys, Kyle and Troy, to school and pick them up at the end of each day, which gave me the chance to speak to their teachers and chart their progress. I had always taken an interest in my children's schooling because my memories of my time at school left a lot to be desired and I did not want my own sons to follow the same path. It transpired that Kyle was perhaps two years in advance of other pupils around him and he was proving to be a very bright individual which filled me with a great deal of satisfaction.

Troy, however, seemed to be going in the opposite direction and I would need to chastise him almost every single day for not appearing to want to put any effort in. It escalated out of control when he began to assault different teachers physically during lessons. I would be requested to come down to the school because Troy would be disrupting the whole class and I was informed that he had stabbed one teacher with a sharpened pencil and ran across the classroom to strike another teacher with a chair. I found this behaviour to be unacceptable and assured the headmistress that I would be having very firm words with him.

I just could not put my finger on the reason why these incidents were becoming so excessive and I even began to question my own parenting skills and blamed myself for the lifestyle I had been living. Troy was given a succession of different teachers and one of them finally realised Troy suffered from a milder form of dyslexia, and given time, it could be corrected.

I had always lied to my children about my schooling and would often tell them I was a very diligent student and I did it for the right reasons regarding them. It will come as a great surprise to them when they now read the true facts.

All Saints School in Nuneaton, which they attended, came under threat of closure at this time and I took it upon myself to write letters of protest to Westminster and also to the local newspapers and it was a campaign that proved fruitful as the school remained open. I am still held in high regard at the school and at a later date I would need to call on the headmistress to provide me with a reference for yet another court appearance and the likelihood of a prison sentence.

I had not always intended to be a bad person. It just seemed my life was to pan out this way, but I was always aware that I had accumulated far more friends than I had enemies. I enjoy the feeling of gaining a lot of respect and admiration throughout my estate and beyond. I am a very approachable person and will champion the cause of any underdog and this is reflected by how warmly people greet me and my children would often be impressed by how many people knew their father. I wanted my children to grow and mature with the exact same principles that I had in life and certainly not to follow the same path as I had done, and so I focused all of my energy on them. I would take them with me everywhere I went and it would raise an eyebrow if I should ever be seen without them.

Night after night I would take upwards of twenty young boys to play football and I suppose all of the parents on the estate would welcome the peace, although Marion would be none too pleased to discover we had additional guests every time a game was over, because all of Kyle's and Troy's friends would ask if they could stay the night, and after I had chosen a few to stay I would need to promise the remaining friends they could stop over on the next occasion.

I think I may have done all of this to maybe compensate for my own childhood that I felt I had missed but I also felt that I needed to do anything that I could to bring Troy back into line.

I had recently been diagnosed with bipolar disorder and I was struggling to come to terms with my own bouts of depression, which were affecting the atmosphere in the home. I would start drifting back to the pub once the children had gone to bed because it seemed that Marion and I were struggling with our relationship and every time we tried to resolve any issues it would end in screaming matches, and I would choose to make for the door rather than be confrontational. If any time was the wrong time for me to resurface from the shadows then this would be the one because cocaine had just become the drug of choice and the area was awash with it.

I had always regarded myself as an individual who had a very high drug tolerance and so I never thought I would encounter many problems. I had mistaken the purity of the drug and felt I would always be in control but I very quickly began to develop a big problem and I would need regular counselling at the Drug Advisory Clinic on Coton Road in Nuneaton. The clinic still remains to this day with the aim of assisting patients, or 'clients' as they prefer to call the visitors. I am quite sure many difficult 'clients' have passed through the doors of the place since it was first established, but I would begin to test their patience to the limits.

After a long weekend of partying, which ended with a large gathering of us up at a local beauty spot called Hatshill Hayes, on the outskirts of Nuneaton, I took the decision to pay a visit to the clinic because I had not been for a long time.

After a long night at an illegal rave perhaps I had chosen an inappropriate time to visit but as I walked past at mid-morning that Monday I did not think I would get the cold greeting that I did. I was told by my counsellor that he felt that the therapy was not working because, out of five appointments made, I had not kept four of them and I had shown up now on a day and at a time when I shouldn't have done.

I argued with him and pointed out that should any individual turn up on the appropriate day and time then they really didn't have a problem with drugs. Whereas my life consisted of madness and mayhem and a regimented routine would be far from my thoughts. He looked rather surprised when I also told him that I was that far removed from reality that I could not even recall what his name was.

It was suggested at regular intervals that I should consider becoming an inpatient at one of our clinics in the town but I was fearful of going into that sort of setting because of my experience when I was younger. But at the same time any forced attendance and being made to reside in any clinic would have hindered my drug taking and I would prefer to continue with the madness and mayhem. Anyone with a drug problem will tell you that they are in full control of the situation and I would be no different and had convinced myself that I would be alright and was not at risk.

I attempted to adhere to my appointment times for a period of time and because my counsellor was about to be re-assigned to a different area I was given a new one and it was stressed to me the importance of building bridges with my latest 'saviour'.

My first appointment was to be the following week and, as always, I had not even blinked my eyes, let alone had a sleep for the best part of three days. I arrived in a complete state of exhaustion and was introduced to a lady with pink and purple hair and a very middle-class manner. It always amazes me that the people given the responsibility of stabilising any of us who have continually abused drugs are no more than textbook specialists, and unfortunately that is not how my world works or the world of many others like me.

After seating me in her office the warmth of the central heating drained the remaining energy I had from me and I slightly nodded off once or twice. Because of my apparent reluctance to speak the lady misread that as a sign of shyness and began to assure me that anything I did or said was strictly confidential within the confines of the four walls of her office. I now did perhaps one of the most foolish things I have ever done and reached for my pocket and spilled a line of powder on her table and swiftly sniffed the contents up my nostrils.

I don't know who was more shocked as I informed her that, if she needed me to speak then unfortunately I was absolutely exhausted and what had just taken place was the only reasonable solution. I did not think that her opinions were of the same mindset as mine as she ushered me out of the door once she had got over the initial shock. Needless to say I was never given any further appointments and my days of receiving counselling had come to an end. I would laugh to myself with the realisation that in no way would the lady have ever been able to read about any incident like that taking place in her textbook degree.

I did not do myself any favours though, and I would need to fall back on help from the medical profession at a later date. I could not have worked if I had wanted to. My life was in a mess and my relationship was hanging by a fine thread but still I refused to believe that I had a major drug problem. My last line of defence should have been the counselling but I had burnt all of my bridges there, and problem or no problem, I would need to deal with it alone.

I was caught in a vicious trap because I was no longer welcome in the family home and found myself spending more and more time in the family pub. My own inner circle would not be aware of the escalating problems I was going through and if ever I appeared to be down, in their eyes the obvious solution would be to give me a wink of the eye and an invitation to the toilets to partake in a little of 'Columbia's Finest Powder' to help me to march along. Above the pub there were some empty bedrooms and I would find myself sleeping there on many occasions when I was not in a fit state to make the short journey home.

I was having a good social life and my drug consumption had increased due to the fact that I would not need to pay my family or their friends any money, and many others maybe welcome that sort of lifestyle, until you consider the disruption in my family life. It is easy now, reflecting back on the days gone by, but as anyone should tell you, in a drug-fuelled existence, selfishness plays a very big part.

I thought of no one but myself and taking drugs on a Tuesday morning would seem just as satisfactory as it would to an occasional user taking drugs on a Saturday evening. One day was no different to any other in my eyes and I would be using drugs on more days in the week than not. I was a disaster waiting to happen. A runaway train without a driver to be seen, and it would only be a matter of time before I derailed.

At this time our pub had to be the craziest place to drink in the whole of the country. It would reach the stage where it was impossible to go to the lavatories, in either the ladies or the gents, to even perform regular toilet duties because yet another line of powder would be placed in front of my face. It would be no exaggeration to say that this procedure would be taking place five or six times throughout a period of an hour and there seemed to be an endless supply of the stuff. If at any time I was left unattended I would casually blow the powder away to grasp at even the slightest respite to try to curtail my consumption.

With the taking of this particular drug it would increase our thirst for alcohol and throughout the day it would become quite easy to drink our way through twenty pints each – how we never had a major casualty in the pub is beyond me.

It just got more insane by the day and while we were drinking one day, a 'madhead' from the nearby town of Bedworth came strolling in like he was out on a Sunday morning walk. His name was Spider and the difference was that he had a double-barrelled shotgun and woke up that morning and decided to come and rob us and our customers at gunpoint. He was distracted by one of the customers and before he knew what was happening he was taken clean out with a punch to his jaw and had the gun taken from him and the butt smashed into him until he was unconscious. He was dragged out of the pub and placed on the grass embankment outside and someone rang for an ambulance anonymously and he would find himself under police guard at the local hospital while he recovered from his injuries. The man must have been on a suicide mission but the legendary status he now has in his hometown may give him a little compensation.

I will inform you shortly that with respect to serious firearms in and around the pub that this incident would be far from an isolated one.

CHAPTER 26

My behaviour was getting more and more erratic. I was in a constant cycle of drug and alcohol abuse and I had once again returned to the all too familiar world of football violence. Maybe I needed an outlet to release all of my tension and football outings seemed to fit the bill.

It was not as if we chose to attend any league games where the police presence would be high. We preferred the quiet setting of non-league football following Nuneaton Borough around the country and on this occasion we would be in Grantham, the home town of the former Prime Minister, Margaret Thatcher. Fortunately we had stayed at a few other areas en route to Grantham and the licensees of the public houses we had visited in Melton Mowbray and Stamford would be prepared to come to court at a later date and testify we had been no problem at all and would have welcomed our custom on the return journey. A journey which would not take place because we would all end up on remand in Lincoln Prison for the next five weeks on trumped-up charges!!

We attended the game in high spirits, and after taking our seats in the stand we began to have a little friendly banter with some of the locals. After a short while a small crowd began to gather towards the rear of us and quite a few cups of hot coffee were thrown in our direction. Believe it or not but on this particular occasion we had not even gone to this game with the intention of causing trouble but we were certainly not the sort to refuse a direct challenge and within seconds a full-blown melee broke out with the end result being more than a few casualties from the ranks of our rival supporters. It got completely out of hand as the crowd spilled onto the pitch and the referee decided to take both sets of players off the pitch for their own safety, and this delayed the game by about half an hour.

We became separated in all of the skirmishes and the police managed to herd us outside the ground. As soon as we got outside I could see my younger brother on the floor and an officer attempting to handcuff Craig. I pushed the officer over and out of the way and managed to rescue Craig, for the time being, but the ever-increasing circle of uniforms insisted he was under arrest for assault. After a long stand-off the police assured us that if we left the immediate area by the ground they would return our brother to us at the earliest opportunity and they suggested that we wait at a public house perhaps five hundred yards from the ground and, foolishly, we agreed to do so.

We had been drinking and playing pool for an hour or more and just remained in the area waiting for our brother to be released. The next time we looked out of the window the pub car park had been completely taken over by the local riot police who were also accompanied by members of the Nuneaton force. They began to bang their shields and created a hostile atmosphere, and snatch-squads ran in at regular intervals to grab any individual that the Nuneaton police pointed out whilst they remained in the rear ranks. It may seem like I am being paranoid but in my family there are six brothers and the five of us that were in attendance would be the first ones to be arrested, even though we had committed no offence. All in all eleven arrests were made and although four would be given bail the police would object to the rest of us having bail and we would find ourselves in Lincoln Prison.

Paddy, Stephen, Glenn, Craig, and myself would be the family members along with Beeston Bill, a known hooligan with banning orders from Leeds, and finally Irish Billy, a good family friend of ours, with a large dragon tattooed all over his face, who would have possibly got bail himself but for the fact that he urinated all over the officers' overcoats which had lain at the back of the van that we had been placed in.

We had a welcoming committee back at the station and by the time I was placed in a cell I was minus a shirt sleeve and had a few cuts and abrasions. Billy, the one who urinated, would be thrown into the cell block like a dart winging its way to the treble twenty on a dart board. Because of the crowded situation we would find ourselves booked in and shunted into the cell block much quicker than normal and the search they had conducted was totally inadequate.

After the cell door was slammed shut I produced a large wrap of amphetamine from my underpants and offered it about to my brothers but they declined. Anyone who takes this drug will tell you of its bitter taste and the need for some fluid to coax the substance down your throat and the only water available was present in the W.C. I flushed the toilet on numerous occasions until I felt that the water looked reasonably clean. Then I placed the powder into my mouth and scooped a handful of the water into my mouth.

I was under the impression we would be bailed in a short while but little did I realise we were to be held in custody all the weekend to appear in court on the Monday morning.

We were crowded three to a cell and I was angry with myself now for not flushing the drug away rather than taking it. I was somewhat hyper and would not get a moment's sleep all night while I watched my two brothers sleep soundly. I spent the night pacing my cell and talking to myself.

Once we had been remanded in custody on the Monday morning our reputation then preceded us because the other inmates had heard, on the local news, of our situation with the riot police. We commanded a lot of respect and the majority of the other prisoners gave us a wide berth and we soon made it clear we were not a group to be messed with. On the group visits that we had, the amount of contraband we could get smuggled in meant we practically ran the black market on the Remand Wing and we lived very comfortably and wanted for nothing.

My only problem was that Marion had chosen not to come on any visit or to even write a letter to me, and I realised it may be over between us. I was embarrassed that I was the only one out of the seven not getting any contact from my partner and it took me back to my early days when I had no one. It should have been a warning but I did not take the gravity of it on board. To make matters worse I was not even guilty of the charges I had been accused of and it would be proven at a later date when I was vindicated.

In Lincoln our younger brother, Craig, would go missing for long periods on the pretext of being bored and he would claim he was going to watch a movie on the bottom landing which would have a screening daily but only in the Remand Wing. The alarm bells were there!! We just had not taken notice of the fact that he was associating with a black lad from Nottingham whose nickname was 'Kit Kat'.

For anyone that is in the know the only silver paper available in any prison canteen shop is the one that envelops a bar of Kit Kat chocolate and it is usually the fastest selling product on the shelf. The silver paper is treasured by the ones who take heroin in the prison because it can be used to 'chase the dragon'.

From that day to the present day our brother has had an ongoing problem with the drug, and we curse ourselves often for not realising what was taking place. The man's name being Kit Kat should have told us all we needed to know, but I suppose we preferred not to believe it. But once we got released on bail we would soon discover how bad the problem had become. Craig and Beeston Bill would not be allowed bail because they had other outstanding charges of assault to answer to. The remaining five of us were granted bail by a judge in chambers after five weeks because I suppose the evidence seemed to just not stack up properly.

After we got out we would continue to visit the remaining two and even though we was smuggling Craig an ounce of cannabis resin on each visit, it would be not enough to maintain his habit and we would need to meet up with 'Kit Kat's wife outside of the jail and give her hundreds of pounds.

When I had finally got home to Marion it was a very strained atmosphere and she refused to believe my claims of innocence. Even when we finally went to court and the decision was reached by the Magistrates not to proceed with a lot of the charges because, in their opinion, the evidence was very scant and insufficient, it would be too late to save my relationship.

We, all of us, knew that the charges would be thrown out. The police from Nuneaton had done what they set out to do and managed to take us off the streets to disrupt the drugs chain that we had developed, but it was not as if we could use that claim to the Magistrates as a sort of mitigating circumstance!!

As an added inconvenience to my brother Paddy, a condition of his bail would be the requirement that he would need to stay in a bail hostel in Leicester. It would be many weeks before the chain could be re-established and the police must have been more than satisfied with the inconvenience they had managed to connive and bring about.

I would need to get myself very busy and I had the ideal opportunity coming up because the Glastonbury festival was due to take place a few weeks later. I purchased a thousand ecstasy tablets for the reasonable sum of eight hundred pounds and I would need to get back to work and build up a pool of money.

Until the introduction of the new super fence at Glastonbury it would be possible to climb in and out on several occasions throughout the weekend and so I would not need to carry the full amount of pills and run the risk of arrest. I would have no more than fifty on my person at any one time, but the captive market of the festival is one not to be missed because the profit margin can be huge.

The easiest outlet is to find the main dance tent and that is where the most likely customers would be. A member of security approached me and informed me that if I shook one more hand I would be shown the exit. After assuring him that it was a friend whom I had not seen since the previous year he once again reiterated, but in a stronger tone, that I was doing 'Trade' and he was not prepared to allow it. I just made myself scarce for a while and resumed my duties later.

Of course I was doing 'Trade'. For Christ's sake!!! My mark-up was immense considering I was paying only eighty pence a pill and selling them for five pounds each or the day's special deal of three for ten pounds.

This way of life had just become second nature to me

and, O.K. I would not exactly ever be chosen to be Alan Sugar's apprentice, but his world is far removed from mine and my career was flourishing again, so I really never had any scruples. We are all consenting adults and if we choose to sell or even take drugs then surely that is our choice and is not to be condemned. In times of conflict all the governments around the world have no qualms about providing certain drugs to the front-line troops but keep placing restrictions on everyday society. It don't wash with me and never has.

If my own government cannot provide me with gainful employment then I will provide my own source of income without any regard to the consequences. All of my family are the same and none of us feel the need to apologise to no one.

I would be at Glastonbury for three or four days at a time and not even see one of the many bands playing on any of the stages because I was there to do my 'work'! Anyone who is a drug dealer will tell you that it requires being able to 'work' around the clock as long as customer satisfaction requires it, and I would need to put in more hours than anyone doing a forty-hour week. I take the risks so why shouldn't I reap the rewards?

Many times throughout my life I have preferred to work, but if that possibility has not been there and my back has been to the wall then I have resorted to other means out of sheer necessity.

I have also been to Glastonbury with limited funds in my pocket and slept rough and queued up at the Hari Krishna tent for free meals when I have been hungry. I know which scenario I prefer and it is not the sleeping rough and begging as I feel I done enough of that as a young buy. I have also attended Glastonbury and rented a six-berth teepee for a staggering amount of sixteen hundred pounds just for a five-day stay. I just marvel at the camaraderie of the place as it turns into a small town without even the slightest hint of trouble. I would recommend it to anyone.

As I was busy in my own sphere my brothers would also need to get the show back on the road and within days of us being cleared of all of the charges related to the football, two of them would be on the ferry and over to Holland. There would be more misfortune waiting though, because apparently the Customs & Excise officers would have the exact same boat marina where my brothers where heading, had some other 'firm' from Liverpool under surveillance at the marina. One brother, feeling uneasy, wisely decided that it may be best if just one of them went it for the 'meet' and he could observe from a distance. In next to no time the marina was surrounded by customs and Dutch police officers and my brother, Stephen, found himself back on remand, albeit in a Dutch prison on this occasion, while matters were investigated further.

Stephen told me on the phone that it was a very relaxed regime and mainly consisted of British prisoners and hardly any Dutch detainees, and just about everyone's offences concerned the importation of drugs.

My other brother managed to get safely back to our shores but Stephen would need to remain where he was for a further six months. How the police back in Nuneaton must have enjoyed the news when it was being relayed to them!!

The tide would soon turn in our direction though, and there would seem to be a never-ending supply of money and we would all be in clover. It would need the forming of a specialist unit of police to try to stem the flow and officers from the West Midlands Serious Crime Squad would be seconded to Nuneaton to investigate the activities of the Ginnelly Empire. We knew of this because of one or two police officers of the time who were corrupt and would keep us in the picture. Money talks in all walks of life and for anyone to not believe that corruption stretches to even the local constabulary, then you have led a very sheltered life!!!

CHAPTER 27

Things were going very well as the large-scale amounts were coming through, and none of us have any problem talking about this period as it has now been and gone and we all know that it is inadmissible as evidence.

Should any consignment not get through and reach its destination then the troubles would begin for anyone who had purchased the load on credit, because for sure the 'wholesaler' would still want his payment. In normal circumstances a purchase of one hundred or more kilos of resin could be transferred to our shores and the recipients would be given two weeks' 'bail' with the produce. It is these transactions based on trust but also a sprinkling of fear, because it would be unwise not to settle outstanding bills with the people involved. Such an amount in a small town such as ours would soon come to the attention of the police and so a network was formed in Coventry, Birmingham, and other outlying areas to dispose of it at a quicker and safer pace.

Our mother, God bless her soul, was given the task of counting out the individual payment bags to determine if anyone was paying in light and skimming off the profits. She enjoyed the task in the early stages, throwing money in the air, as we often do when we came into contact with large amounts of money we were unaccustomed to handling. The novelty would soon wear off with her while she sat in the seclusion of her bedroom needing to count up to three hundred thousand pounds at a time, on a weekly basis, as the workload increased markedly. It may seem the job made of dreams but if our mother was here to tell the story she would tell you that it was definitely not the case. Our mother was one of us and a serious 'mother hen' who saw no wrong in what any of us did.

She had been to Pucklechurch Prison herself on two occasions and she would never be ashamed to tell people of this because she revelled in being a part of it all. We were like the cast of the TV programme 'BREAD' and the only thing that would be missing would be the ornament of the hen on the table for us all to place money in. I became very close to my mum and loved her totally, and admired how her own life had been difficult but she had survived. Mrs. G. was famous nationwide as our mother and she would be adorned with jewellery on every part of her. If ever a lady merited the title 'THE GODMOTHER' then this lady was the one.

If ever a large group of friends were visiting from Yorkshire no one was permitted to go back up the Motorway until they had been given a Sunday dinner and we have known her to feed twenty-odd different people in four sittings. She would simply ring 'The Donni' and instruct another six to make their way over after the previous sitting had eaten their lunch. She was a remarkable lady and KATHLEEN GINNELLY is a part of folklore in Nuneaton as many people will testify. I will speak in detail about our mother shortly.

We had money coming out of our ears and the champagne and cocaine lifestyle could begin in earnest as we all lived the dream a little. The only wrong turning we had seemed to have taken was when our friend Steve Craythorne had been caught in a sting and sentenced to ten years' imprisonment but we never let him go without and we would need to drive down to Dartmoor to visit him.

It seemed very much like our cards had been marked and if we did not show a little more caution then we would end up joining our friend Steve on his exercise yard. The decision was taken to 'drop anchor' for a while and place all of our activities on hold.

It was during this period that we discovered our father had been diagnosed with a terminal throat cancer and it proved to be a very difficult time. Our mother did what any loving partner would do and took the decision to have 'Dan' at home to see out his final days. The family would need to pull together because our mother was struggling more and more to come to terms with what was occurring. It would be the first time I would witness what a devastating illness cancer can be and I can honestly say it would be the last way I would choose to exit this world. I would rather go through the windscreen of a car and have an instantaneous death than the long, painful demise our father went through. After the expert medical opinion is given as to how long the sufferer can be expected to survive, the calculations, more often than not, prove to be correct.

Dan's death tore our family apart for a while and as in any large family all of us would handle our grief in different ways, but our mother was totally heartbroken. We would never be given the chance to see our mum in all of her confident glory again, as she just gave up on life herself and retired to bed early each night, reading books about the afterlife. We would attempt to take her out socialising but at the earliest chance she would make her way back to the family home, preferring to be alone with her memories.

The local Council would give our mother the added worry of losing her five-bedroomed property due to the fact that Dan had died and they were insistent that she vacated her home of forty-years to accommodate a larger family. The constant flow of letters from the Council were the last thing our mum needed at this tragic time and the only other option available would be to purchase the property at a great reduction in its true value because of the family's long term of residency.

The money was garnished together by whatever means and after weeks of needless, heartless worry created by the Council, our mother became the owner of the home but it would be scant compensation for the loss of her 'soulmate'.

We got our mum a small dog, which she named after Dan, in the hope that she had a little company to assist in alleviating her pain and loss at such a difficult time, but it was a loss that she would never fully recover from.

At the time, Dan's death brought me and Marion a little closer but I think we both knew we was just papering over the cracks and there would be no way back. My mum would try to push us back closer together but it was inevitable I suppose that we would split.

Marion had discovered about a little 'fling' I had gone through with another woman about eighteen months previous, and that would be the final nail in my coffin.

All of us have regrets in life and this one would be my 'cross to bear'. I have never forgiven myself for the disruption I must have caused to my children's lives and progress in it, but none of us can ever be given the chance to turn the clock back. Life is a learning process and all of us have to stand or fall by the decisions we make and I readily admit I made some wrong choices. I am not about to throw mud but I was about to be made to endure something that no father should be put through with the absence of my children.

I took the decision to leave the home Marion and I had shared for ten years, after the arguments continued unabated and they appeared to be having an affect on the children.

I would still maintain regular contact and the best feeling any man could ask for is the sight of the youngest child running and jumping into one's arms as Demi would often do. Kyle and Troy had taken the separation in their stride and at the times of contact would simply show up with their football ready for our regular knockabout. But with Demi it would be different! She was four years old and so cute and pretty and such a loving little girl. Any father will confirm that there is no better feeling for a father than a daughter hanging from one's neck.

I tried to correct my way of life and would very shortly obtain work, but it would be much too late to salvage anything from my relationship with Marion and I would spend much of my time with a very heavy heart and in a state of depression. To raise my spirits I decided to make my annual pilgrimage to Glastonbury, but this would be a festival I would long remember for all of the wrong reasons.

I had made my way down to Pilton Farm in Somerset on the Friday evening and scaled the fence as I had done on many previous occasions because, as always, I was without a ticket. Not long after getting into the grounds I had managed to lose all of my friends due to my drug-induced state, but it mattered little to me as I never had any problem introducing myself to complete strangers and forming a bond. If I came across my original friends throughout the festival period then so be it, but I would be aware of where we had parked the vehicle so I would link up with them prior to our departure from the area.

I purchased some very strong ecstasy tablets with the name tag 'ELEPHANTS'. I suppose the name had come about because of the enormity of the tablets and they would need to be swallowed half a tablet at a time. These particular tablets were of a very potent nature and I drifted around the festival aimlessly in a very pleasant state of mind. If anyone has ever been to Glastonbury you would appreciate the vastness of the crowd and how it is virtually impossible to locate anyone you might need to meet.

It was mid-morning on the Saturday and I just drifted into the field that had a load of large wigwams erected and, miraculously, caught sight of my sister, Susan, with a bench set-up trading Crystal Healing Stones. We rejoiced at coming across each other and marvelled at how it had come about in such a large crowd, but stranger things were about to take place. We had no sooner sat down and engaged in a little conversation when a group of people we knew from our home town appeared on the horizon. They had been given the task of finding both me and Susan in order to relay some information and they doubted they would find even one of us, let alone locating the pair of us, together!

Susan and I would never take mobile phones to a festival because the whole purpose of going would be to escape from the trials and tribulations of our own local town, but we were about to learn that, at such times as this, a means of contact is essential. As the group approached us we could sense the nervous tension as no one wished to be the bearer of the news, instead preferring to pass us the phone and it was our brother Paddy's voice we were about to hear. The phone was passed to me and Patrick asked me to sit down and prepare myself. As he spoke I glanced over in the direction of Susan and could instantly see tears streaming down her face and I realised the very same news had just been relayed to her.

Our mother had been found dead that morning after

taking a tumble and banging her head. I was completely dumbstruck and also ashamed of myself for being in such a drug-induced state while I was listening to this heartbreaking news. I poured a bottle of skunk scrumpy cider over my head to try to wake up my senses a little and clear my head but the ecstasy I had taken had my brain and my train of thought in a serious state of disrepair.

Paddy suggested that we should perhaps remain at the festival because we could not change the situation, but no way could we even attempt to become involved in the festival and all its entertaining activities.

The decision was taken that Susan and I, along with her daughter, Angela, and Susan's boyfriend of the time, Thommo, should make the long journey home. After discussions with a few of the Glastonbury stewards, arrangements were made for us to gain access to the car park by means of a shortcut through one of the private areas.

We drove into the town of Glastonbury and purchased some very nice candles to light for our mother once we got home. I can honestly say that no journey has ever in my whole life appeared to take as long to complete. The silence was deafening, and I can recall little to nothing about any conversation that took place on that fateful day. I could sense the love in the car from my sister Susan, and she would feel the same as we both grieved in silence.

Once we arrived back at Susan's home we lit the candles and had a few visits from our other siblings and never had we thought this day would come around so closely after Dan's death. Towards the end of the evening I could take no more and needed to take my mind away onto a different level, and so I left Susan's home and dropped a trip of acid I had in one of my pockets. Round the back of the estate in Hilltop lies an all-night garage and a dual carriageway and my night was spent hallucinating the hours away. To any regular person it may seem an inappropriate thing to do but it was my way of dealing with it. I was just as heartbroken as anyone and my loss felt immeasurable. Yes we had got off to a bad start in life but I had finally, in later years, done a lot of bonding and I learnt to love my mother as any son would. My mother was a true 'one-off'. Loved and admired my many and the three thousand pounds worth of flowers at her funeral would be testimony to that.

This period in my life would have a serious effect on the state of my health, both physically and mentally. In the space of eighteen months I had lost my mother, stepfather, partner, and children. These were not minor mishaps. These were major tragedies that it seemed I would never recover from as I would descend into a deep black depression requiring treatment as an in-patient at the local psychiatric hospital.

The emptiness I felt plunged me into a very black hole and I became a very unbalanced person who would need transporting by my doctor to the hospital while I laid in the back of his car with a blanket placed over me. I would need to stay in hospital for many weeks to come, all the time receiving treatment.

CHAPTER 28

Our mum's entourage for her funeral would be perhaps the biggest ever assembled in Nuneaton, as people attended from every area of the country to pay their respects and the church could have been filled three times over. The traffic in the centre of the town was held up for forty minutes to allow us to pass through and mum would have been very amused by the horses, from her carriage, defecating directly outside the police station. This would be the talking point of the day as it presented a little light relief to the proceedings.

All of the brothers were given the proud opportunity to carry our mother's coffin in and out of the church, except he youngest who would be escorted to the funeral by two prison officers, who refused steadfastly to remove the handcuffs even though we constantly assured them there would be no attempt at escaping. I think our mother would have found it quite amusing that the pews accommodating the family would also contain two prison officers because all of our various existences seemed to have incorporated either police officers or warders.

I had needed the love of my children around me at this particular time and, rather foolishly, when I was drunk, I had breeched the terms of my contact with the children. I had been made to have contact with them through legal channels and to visit a centre for a period of time and build up to be allowed regular home visits. I found it all very distasteful to stand in front of a judge, who knew nothing of my parenting skills, and need to ask for permission to take my children on holiday to Butlins, and yet this is what it had come to.

I was in a very bad place psychologically at this time and was having great difficulty coming to terms with my mood swings, which could stretch from one end of the Grand Canyon to the other in diversity. It would prove very hard at those times I was denied access to my children, because as any concerned father should tell you it is like having ribs missing from your body. I breached the access I had been given on a few occasions and found myself in front of the judge in respect of not keeping to the terms of my injunction. I was astounded that no one in authority could appreciate the recent family bereavements and my set of circumstances, but I would not receive one bit of sympathy from this judge as he gave me a term of imprisonment, albeit suspended.

I should have heeded the warning but rather than do so I once again found myself within two hundred yards of an area I was not permitted to enter. I had just gone through all of the trauma I had, and considering I had spent twelve years with Marion I would have expected her to show just a little consideration, but I would be wrong. I was tracked down and arrested to be stood in front of the judge the following morning and of course I have a lot of resentment towards any parent who can place the other parent in this type of predicament, but this is the wrong place to air those views.

I was the father of the children and yet it seemed I was deemed to be not needed in their lives. The judge looked even less kindly on me as he sentenced me to eight weeks in Winson Green Prison in Birmingham. I was in a state of shock when I arrived in the prison, as I had not been in this place for many a year. A lot of women on the estate were up in arms at what had happened to me and had begun a petition at the local shop.

I did not know it at the time but Marion had used my enforced absence as an opportunity to leave the area, and I was never to see my children again.

In the prison I had other pressing matters to deal with as I was placed in a cell with a disturbed Muslim. I had noted from his card he had come from the medical wing and he constantly prayed and splashed water on every stride I was taking in the cell. This can only be amusing for a certain period of time, and after a while it becomes very annoying and tiresome, especially if the routine is still on-going into the early hours of the morning.

The Muslim had not even spoken one word to me and I was unsure as to whether he could even speak English, but as I got out of my bed and pressed the emergency button, he enquired, "Are you going somewhere?" I assured him I was not going anywhere and in actual fact it was he that was leaving!

The night watchman sympathised with my complaint but informed me nothing could be done until the morning. For the remainder of the night my Muslim friend would stare at me menacingly and I chose not to get back into my bed, being fearful that I may get my throat cut if I slept.

How the fuck had I landed in here after all my years of freedom? And it was definitely not doing my depression any favours!!

I was moved to a different cell in the morning because as soon as the cell door was opened I stood on the landing with all of my kit and belongings and refused point blank to go back in. I would have preferred going down into solitary on a disciplinary charge and I think the wardens knew this, so they resolved the matter by moving me along to a different cell.

I found myself in the company of a certain Paul Wood from Kingstanding in Birmingham. Paul was looking at a very long sentence because he had been arrested on firearms offences having returned to a pub called 'The Kingstanding Arms' to settle a score. The bouncer at the pub had beaten Paul up earlier in the evening, but he had gone back when the doorman was at the end of his shift and fired a shotgun into one of the bouncer's knees. I found Paul to be a very good cellmate and neither of us would have any inclination to 'pray to the East' and the memory of the manic Muslim would soon fade away.

Winson Green had taken a turn for the worse since my previous visit when I was serving my three year sentence and there was a serious problem with the misuse of heroin being top of the list. Paul and I would prefer to spend our evenings smoking cannabis and exchanging anecdotes with each other.

Every person creates their own problems with drugs, because inmates prefer taking heroin – it can be passed through the body much quicker by urinating, whereas cannabis remains in one's system much longer. Considering that frequent drug tests take place the inmates prefer to take heroin safe in the knowledge they have a much easier chance to pass the test, but this system creates far more addicts once they are released. It is a strange situation but it appears the Home Office prefer to bury their heads in the sand on this matter and deny there is a problem.

I could not wait to get out of this prison and even

though the stay was a short one it would be a sharp reminder to me that, should I choose to live this way, there would always be a bed made available to me. I didn't know it at this time but this would be the last term I ever spent in a prison and I never felt I would ever be able to say that!! My life would still be full of drama, but my penal career would finally come to an end.

Because I was considered a 'civil' prisoner as opposed to a 'criminal' one, I was permitted to spend a great deal more money at the prison canteen than the other prisoners and this would benefit Paul and I greatly. When the day came for my release I left Paul with all of my worldly possessions and assured him that I was not the sort of person to promise to post goods into the prison and then not do it. I, more than anyone, knew the importance of receiving contact from the outside world and knew the feeling it generates, having mail or parcels with magazines delivered to the cell, and I would honour my promises to Paul.

Anyone who knows me personally will confirm that I correspond with anyone at all who I know to be in any institution. I have done this my entire life and it would be no exaggeration to claim I have sent thousands of parcels and letters to different individuals, male or female, in just about every prison around the country.

I kept in touch with Paul after his release and we even had the good fortune to meet up with each other at Glastonbury many years later. The last information I received about Paul was that he had had the misfortune to come across some of the doorman's friends and they gave him a severe beating and put him in hospital. I wish you well my friend, wherever you are now.

I was released from Winson Green Prison just as we entered the millennium and with the turn of the century I hoped my life would take a turn for the better, but it was not to be. On arriving back in Nuneaton I looked forward to the prospect of, once again, seeing my children, who I had missed sorely, but I was informed that they no longer lived in the area and no one had a clue as to their whereabouts.

I was devastated and at a loss as to what to do. I was thankful to our local newspaper for reporting the matter and allowing me to place a photographed appeal in the next edition. I also printed out my own personal appeals and got most of the local shops to place the posters in their shop windows.

I was sleeping on different people's settees throughout the estate but I would be good company for no one as I became completely inconsolable. As each week passed with no information at all I became quite ill with worry and I would not wish this on my worst enemy to endure. Foolishly I turned to much harder drugs – it was very rare that I had woken up craving anything in the past, but that was about to change.

I had been offered the chance to inject myself with heroin, but I declined, instead preferring to 'chase the dragon' by smoking the drug through a tube while I melted it on silver foil. Heroin was not a drug that would agree with me and I would be violently sick on the occasions that I took it, and by now the new kid on the block, crack cocaine, had arrived and I fell into the natural progression of sampling its effects. I enjoyed it a little too much and soon began to develop a bit of a problem with the euphoric state it would put me in, but the depression would return and the problem of my missing children would intensify.

I am not an expert and none of us can explain the addled state our brains get into, but I seemed to be so alone in my grief that there seemed only one way out and that was to hang myself. I now try to bury this incident in my subconscious and have great difficulty even discussing it, but after this failed suicide attempt I found myself heavily sedated and in a secure psychiatric unit. The drug I was taking at the time would not have helped my judgement in any way and I very soon realised that I was being kept in the right place.

Of course it was embarrassing that I was needing to be treated for mental issues again but once I had accepted that these issues needed addressing, I was fine about my stay in hospital. I became very reclusive and remained in my 'room' a lot of the time, preferring not to discuss the recent events that had taken place. I was trying to come to terms with it myself and needed to determine for myself what had driven me to such extreme action. I am not ashamed to admit that I cried a river during this period while I tried to come to terms with what had taken place. I did not even venture out of the hospital to the local shop for essentials, and preferred staying in the communal television room and the sanctuary that it offered.

I would have visits from my family and after a few weeks one of my brothers convinced me that I was on the mend and seemed to be my old self again, and took me out of the hospital, drove me to my sister's home, and left me there. I was anxious all through the night and it soon became clear that by not having my medication I was having a difficult time of it. An emergency call was made and I would soon be back in the safe confines of my room and I would squeeze my pillow like it was a new born baby with the relief of being 'home'. I would need many more weeks of treatment and whilst I remained in there some of the senior medical staff would set about coming to some arrangement with the local council to provide me with a two-bedroomed flat in my own community which I still occupy to this day.

I am no criminal psychologist and no expert psychiatrist, and if I could bring my condition to a satisfactory conclusion tomorrow then I would, but I have been told, unfortunately, I will probably always suffer from this condition.

Depression can be a terrifying illness and I would much rather have a physical ailment than be constantly getting lost in the maze of my mind. Was I destined to be this way or did all of the events that unfolded in my life contribute or even create the illness? It is not for me to determine the cause and it appears there is no solution, so it appears that I have to live with this illness.

But for now, my counsellors and doctors had got me a new home and I would have something to target my energies but, as always, the shortage of any monetary funds would bring things to a standstill. I was in my home for a month and all I had was a camp bed, a radio alarm and a kettle. I knew I needed to motivate myself but my mental state was a hindrance as I would always be depressed and very fatigued. I assured my doctors I was going in the right direction and pleased with my flat because I did not want to end up back in the hospital.

My family had begun to shun me a little because of my state of mind and I would not even be welcome in my brother's pub, 'The Donni'. I was barred on two different occasions because if ever I entered the premises no one would wish to make eye contact with me because of my erratic behaviour. I would spend long, lonely days in my unfurnished home with no visitors and my whole thought process would be very negative.

Until someone has woken up one day and discovered that there is no likelihood of seeing their children again, they have no right to judge my behaviour at that time. I was on heavy medication and I had just recovered from a serious drug addiction, but in no way am I trying to condone my behaviour, because I would need to deal with all of these matters all alone. It was a very difficult period in my life and I hope all of you, from around that time, appreciate that I did not intend to offend any of you.

I am a much stronger individual now but that period was a serious test of my character and I almost drowned while I was swimming in my own tears. I had lost both parents, my partner, my children, and my family home. I had a very big crisis but I survived it all and I am still here, thankfully, to tell the story.

CHAPTER 29

While I was barred from the pub I managed to get myself some work, through an agency, at various warehouses throughout the area and all seemed to be going well.

Whenever I could not go into the pub it would give me the chance to avoid the drugs that had caused so many problems for me, and that would be a big bonus while I was trying to bring some normality back into my life.

My surname would always create problems in the job market and the agency would be asked regularly if they were aware I was from a notorious family, and if they could vouch for me personally. It should not have happened because it is a form of discrimination, but unfortunately it did. All I could do was keep my head down, do my work, and hope to impress, which I finally did, and was given a full-time work placement at a large Tesco distribution warehouse in Hinckley in Leicestershire just over the border from where I live. I would remain there for the next four years but I do not know how I survived considering all of the drama that was about to unfold.

My next-door neighbours in my block of flats were a middle-aged couple who I knew quite well and I would often have a glass or two of cider with them. They would have lots of domestic squabbles with each other and at these times I would make myself scarce. So it was no surprise to come home in the early hours one morning and find a large police presence on the landing. I jokingly asked which one of them had killed the other but they told me, in a very earnest manner, they were not prepared to divulge any information at this moment in time.

As if I care, I thought to myself as I slammed my door in the face of the officers and proceeded to my bed, taking no notice of their remarks. If I had taken the time to have noticed I would have seen that some of the officers had bullet-proof vests on and were part of a very serious firearms unit.

I slept soundly through the night and was a little surprised to find that the officers were still around in the morning, and I noted immediately that a few of them seemed to be armed. I light-heartedly implied that I had spoken to some of the other residents and we all felt comforted by the police presence, because it was a neighbourhood were we did not even feel safe enough to venture out to the corner shop. The officer stared at me coldly and I am sure he felt that in some way I was aware of what they had discovered in the adjoining flat.

As I went to pass him in order to go and purchase some cigarettes from the shop he told me that it would be better if no one went anywhere right now as they were about to conduct door-to-door enquiries. I came back to my flat and felt that this must be a murder enquiry with the amount of police in attendance. I could hear some of them rummaging about and because it was a hot summer's day I went back out and shouted through the letter box, "It must be like an oven in there. Can I get you lads an ice cream?" It did not go down too well and I was told if I interfered one more time I would be placed under arrest.

This all seemed very grave and I was intrigued as to what had taken place. One of my brothers rang me and informed me that I should get out of the area as soon as I could because the police had discovered a gun cache in the flat. Apparently an Uzi sub-machine gun and a thousand rounds of ammunition along with some handguns had been found in a holdall and, very strangely, a rhino horn was also in the bag.

I was not prepared to face any awkward questions, so, after assuring one of the officers that I was only going to the shop to purchase a few items, and I would be back straight away, I made good my escape and I would not return to the area for the next few weeks.

It transpired the couple next door had one of their many arguments, and the daughter from a previous relationship had run out of the flat to warn her birth father to be careful because guns were in the flat. A taxi driver, on hearing this, had radioed for the police.

They were both remanded in custody and would be sentenced for refusing to name who the guns actually belonged to.

We all thought it quite amusing at the time that the rhino horn was valued at ten thousand pounds even then in the court room. Recently I read an article stating that in the present year of 2014 a rhino horn is estimated to be worth two hundred thousand pounds. It is used in many Far Eastern countries as a form of medication and as an aphrodisiac.

Armed police would patrol the estate for a long time after that incident and it was clear to see that local officers had become unnerved by the realisation that even a small area such as ours had, overnight, become heavily armed. Specialist Investigation Units had been drafted in and our pub had now 'registered' on the radar as a very prolific target and it had to be closed down at all costs.

The two people caught with the guns would suffer the consequences of their actions but would adhere to their code of conduct and refuse to implicate others. It was rumoured that they were given a certain amount of money each week to 'babysit' the armoury.

It would not be too long before a large scale operation involving two or three forces converged on the pub with the intention of finding any evidence at all to enable them to oppose the re-issue of the license and thus close the premises.

Unfortunately a handgun was found in the safe that sat in the corner of the office. It had either been forgotten about or perhaps no one had wanted to attempt to smuggle it out of the estate in the preceding weeks because of the greater police numbers.

It was also apparent that there was no correct license for the poker gaming machines and, behind the bar, the police claimed they had discovered books and ledgers with names and amounts indicating that some money lending had been taking place. In actual fact they were no more than a list of who owed what for beer they had not paid for on earlier occasions, but the police wanted to draw their own conclusions and needed to build up a case for closing the place. They would be granted the powers to close the pub and, before any appeals could be lodged, arrangements had been made by the brewery to level the place and build a block of flats on the site. 'The Donni' has now become a block of respectable flats for single mothers.

The pub is a well-missed meeting place for all of us on the estate and a stronghold that has been very difficult to replace. The police, however, were very satisfied with the outcome and we heard stories of drinks, toasting and high-fiving down in the police canteen at the station. We would need another pub, and one preferably in close proximity to the estate, but for the time being some serious tragedies were about to take place.

I mentioned earlier in the book about the murder of a very good friend of ours and a regular customer in 'The Donni', but it still rankles me to this day that the police never brought anyone to book for the offence. James Fenton, or 'Irish Jim' as he preferred to be called, was a loveable rogue and I do not feel that he deserved the end that he met.

He obviously trusted the person that was sat in the back of his car and travelling with him, but in a typical gangland execution he would be shot in the back of the head whilst he parked his car.

I would like to think that the death was investigated thoroughly but I am not sure this was the case, and a certain apathy to the case made me feel the police thought that if any of us 'lived by the sword', then it was fine by them if we also 'died by it'!!! We had had a lot of tragedy amongst us and the feeling was that surely it must now come to an end. That was until the weekend we travelled down to Bournemouth to watch Nuneaton Borough in an F.A. Cup tie.

As we had always done when the opportunity arose to visit a Football League Club's ground, there would be in excess of five thousand of our supporters going to the game. It would prove to be a very eventful day and a party atmosphere ensued as we took over all of the pubs in this coastal area.

Inside of the ground we filled the away section to its full capacity and the heavy-handed approach of the Dorset police would create a very hostile atmosphere and a few of our friends would be snatched and placed under arrest and put in the detention vans outside of the ground. All of us were in high spirits and when we noticed some of the detainees were being brought back into the ground to use the urinals we surrounded the officers and 'reclaimed' the prisoners and set about changing their appearance by giving them alternative clothing. We teased and taunted the police all day long and they would later claim we were the worst group of supporters it had ever been their displeasure to meet. We had an altercation with the police outside of the ground and we refused to join the escort out of town until our one last detainee was released, and after we informed them we would 'play up' for the remainder of our stay they took the decision to release the prisoner on the proviso that we left the area.

All of this confrontation had delayed us to the extent we would be miles behind our other friends on the Motorway, although we were still in contact with them via our mobile phones. We had arranged to rendezvous at any small town on the way back to break up our journey and it didn't cause us any concern when we could no longer contact our friends as we simply believed they were now settled in some pub en route.

Unfortunately we had begun to hear rumours of a minibus being involved in a crash involving fatalities. We had stopped at Newbury in Berkshire and our continued pleas to the officers of that area fell on deaf ears because they said the next of kin had not been notified. After a few urgent phone calls from us back to our own hometown we would eventually discover that Martin Lashley, Cal Long and Shaun Folan had been declared dead at the scene and the other occupants of the minibus had suffered serious injuries after the bus, due to a fault in the breaking system, had careered down a Motorway embankment. These boys had always been very good friends to me and I would never be able to forget the date as the accident happened on my birthday, the ninth of December. Since that day I have always felt a little guilty celebrating my birthday as I am close to all of the family members left behind and I feel some of their loss.

Our club has formed close bonds with Bournemouth Football Club since that fateful day and a sponsored cycle-ride has taken place from their ground all the way to Nuneaton's ground, with them arriving in time for the kick-off of that particular day's match. None of these lads will ever be forgotten and we have regular events to commemorate them.

I also had the added grief of one of the victims, Shaun Folan, being my ex-partner Marion's brother. I was still unaware of where my children had been taken to, and I felt that attending Shaun's funeral with the intention of finding out any information, would neither be the right time nor the place to do it.

The tragedy did not end there because one of the lad's close friends, Oscar, could not come to terms with what happened and decided to take his own life by hanging himself.

These young men will always be remembered in Nuneaton Borough F.C. folklore and in our latest pub, Kelly's Bar, a signed football shirt from all the Nuneaton players has pride of place hanging on the main wall of the pub.

REST IN PEACE boys. Your memory will go on forever in our hearts and minds.

CHAPTER 30

The events that had taken place after the Bournemouth game had left a bad taste in my mouth and I had had enough of football for a while. Because of a few unruly incidents that had taken place in Newbury on our way home the police had studied CCTV footage and arrived in Nuneaton to do the customary early morning raids. What was wrong with these people? Of course our behaviour may have been a little excessive! But we had just lost three of our close friends and all of the survivors of the crash would be in the hospital for many months to come. I would have expected a little sympathy and compassion but it would not be forthcoming. My brother, Stephen, and a friend, Michael Taylor, would find themselves having to serve six months in Oxford Prison. The game was up now as far as attending football matches as CCTV had put paid to all of that, and any trouble would soon be nipped in the bud. As far as I was concerned it was time to call it a day and find an alternative pastime.

I would soon settle back into the festival circuit and Glastonbury would always remain my favourite as it gave me the chance to stand in the exact same spot where I had been notified of my mother's death. I would sit in silence for a while and say a quick prayer and then proceed to get absolutely wasted for the duration of my stay.

I would also enjoy going to the Summer Solstice at Stonehenge, although on one particular visit I would come into contact with the Thames Valley Riot Police, who can be very brutal. Apparently legislation had been passed preventing members of the public from accessing the site, which I felt was very unfair considering it is part of our heritage.

As we drew nearer to the area I had already been told over my mobile phone that a large police presence was clearly in view and they were being heavy handed towards the peaceful protestors. After parking I noticed this for myself and noted that the officers held small round shields in their hands. I knew instantly that these would be utilised in any hand-to-hand combat when they finally took the decision to clear the area. These officers have been responsible for some of the worst violence meted out to passive demonstrators for many years and, to this day, can be seen at the forefront of any gathering that the authorities feel may require dispersing. The shield would be used to keep anyone at arm's length while the free hand would be wielding a baton to bring down on anyone who dared question their authority.

I thought it ironic that I had left the world of football violence and yet here I was, in the midst of the most feared police unit in the country, who had no qualms about beating any of us about the head or body. These people are a law unto themselves and seem answerable to no one.

My sister and I began to run across some fences, closely pursued by a few of the riot police and I can recall my sister, Susan, shouting to me to keep running and asking me if I could feel the power of the Stones and insisting I must touch them. The 'power' of the stones is not something that interests me that much, being as how I was only there to be involved in the festival. I did as my sister asked and ran for my life, but the only 'power' that concerned me was sensing the 'power' that one of those batons could do to my head, and if need be I would not only run towards the stones but straight past them to avoid any contact with the fast-approaching police. Normally one thousand football hooligans would stand toe-to-toe with these bastards, but on this day it would be lots of peace-minded hippies running around and scooping their children up as they screamed for help.

'Gentlemen' of the Thames Valley Police, may I say I could NEVER salute your heroics. Some of your riot unit would have included the very same people that policed the North during the miners' strike in the eighties, and your actions disgust me and I am sure that lots of members of the public who have had the misfortune to come across you would feel the exact same way. We left the site at Stonehenge after witnessing some of the worst brutality ever.

On our next excursion we headed up the M1 to Leeds where a large festival called THE LOVE PARADE was being held in Roundhay Park. The problem for the organisers is that no one can safely calculate just how many people are likely to attend as opposed to a pre-paid festival with tickets already sold. On this occasion three hundred thousand would show up and even though it rained all through the day and night none of us would be going anywhere as we were waiting for the headlining D.J. Sasha from Liverpool to start performing.

Years after, at another free event, this time in Brighton on the South Coast, about half a million people showed up for a beach party put on by the D.J. Fat Boy Slim. The event was the best I would ever attend and cars would be abandoned everywhere. It took us three hours to drive the last seven miles into Brighton as there were such great long traffic tailbacks. Unfortunately two people were crushed to death and the Brighton and Hove council have never allowed the event to take place again. Norman Cook a.k.a. Fat Boy Slim was born in Brighton, and there are not many celebrities who give something back, but he decided to stage the event as a reward to all of his supporters. So a big THANK YOU from me Fat Boy because that one weekend could never be matched and I am sure all of us in attendance will never forget it.

But, back to Leeds and Roundhay Park. I had arranged to meet up with my eldest son, David, as I always did if I was in the area. A few of us had gone up in a Bedford van and a few young ladies from Nuneaton had accompanied us up there. My son fell in love with one of them and Nicola and David became inseparable and eventually she would move up to the area to live with him. Not surprisingly, as a result of all this romance I would soon be put in the proud position of becoming a grandfather for the first time to a beautiful little girl called Kadi Mae. Surely this was to be the turning point in my life and I would need to purchase some slippers and a pipe!!!

I would also discover at this time that I was not a well man, and I would have a double reason to have an enforced retirement. Because of my many years of drug abuse, and in particular the chemical elements side of things, I was diagnosed with a very serious hiatus hernia. I would have a great deal of discomfort and it would be virtually impossible to sleep through the night because I would be vomiting blood at regular intervals. After repeated visits and stays in hospital the final decision would be taken for me to have keyhole surgery to correct the hernia. It was explained to me that the side effects would mean I could never be sick again or even burp, but the wind would need to escape somewhere.

I took this to mean I would now be a boring old man that would stand at many a bar, regaling people with my stories, passing wind constantly. There was no escaping the fact that the operation was necessary, and so I signed the papers and received the surgery at Walsgrave Hospital in Coventry and it was a complete success.

I had previously burnt my oesophagus out to such an extent that this operation would need to be done and common sense should have prevailed with the wake-up call I had just received. I should have taken it on board that I could no longer be the 'Peter Pan' of the drug world, but instead I chose the other path and it was not long before 'normal service' resumed. It was like I had been given a second lease of life and I took full advantage of it, and to be quite truthful, I still do so to this day.

Not long after the operation I did the most stupid thing I have ever done in my whole life. I had a few complications and I would need to have one of my tonsils removed at the same hospital, and even though I knew I was to be in the operating theatre the following morning, I foolishly stayed up all night taking cocaine. After being placed under sedation I could remember clearly sitting up during the operation and demanding to know what was occurring. I was pushed back down and I presume I was given additional anaesthetic. When I questioned the incident later I was assured by a member of the surgeon's team that this had not taken place and many patients would say they had woke during an operation, and that it was a regular occurrence for a patient to feel this way.

How dare I even question what had taken place. I know for sure it did actually happen but I also knew I had been taking a Class A substance all the previous night and right up to two hours prior to arriving at the hospital. I could have died that day and my stupidity had no bounds, but it was a sharp reminder of how my drug abuse was careering out of control once again.

By now my brothers had, by whatever means, purchased a much smaller pub that had previously been run as a wine bar and everything would be almost the same as it was before, drinking till the early hours or even through the night. Strangely enough I think the police preferred knowing exactly where we were again and having all of us under the same roof because since they had closed 'The Donni' we had all been split up and all over the town in different pubs.

Business carried on as usual but these were the days when cocaine had devastated all of our lives, and it reached the stage where every one of the 'brothers' was now leading the life of single men. None of us could even begin to blame the women because we had done the damage ourselves by staying out night after night and preferring the company of a bag of cocaine!

I do not know how true it is but the wine bar had been owned previously by a homosexual couple, and the rumour was that due to its prime location and close proximity to our estate they had been forced to leave. I was told that after repeated offers to purchase the pub, all of them declined, a few windows were broken from time to time until it reached the stage where the owners felt obliged to sell, and it would be at a vastly reduced price.

The pub was run by our brother Jimmy who never at any time got involved in the criminal side of things, although he would be aware of certain things we got up to and he would turn a blind eye. Jimmy is a well-known figure in non-league football as a well-respected manager who has run a succession of prominent football clubs. He is the only member of the family who has no criminal past or convictions but, if the need ever arose for us all to stand shoulder to shoulder to protect our 'business interests', then he could be relied upon to stand alongside the rest of us.

I had begun to get some semblance of order in my home at last, compared to how sparsely furnished it had been before. I had now got a job closer to home and was employed at a Lynx distribution warehouse. Whenever I got the chance to redirect my life I would seize the opening gladly, even though the wages in a warehouse would be less than I had been earning twenty-five years previously in the steel industry.

I was always of the opinion that, should any of my children ever resurface, I would prefer them to see their father in a different light to what they had possibly been told about me. I would hold this job down for the next seven years, until I was made redundant, even though I was partying very hard all throughout the period. Often my friends would be doing the security at all of the big music festivals, and therefore I would not need to have a ticket or pay to enter any of these big venues. Of course I should have by now 'dropped anchor' and led a much more quiet and stable life, but once the phone rang and I was given the offer to attend a festival, I would never need asking twice.

It would not do me any favours being in my flat alone with my dated photographs of my children, who I had not seen for many years now. There had been times when I had smashed to bits what little furniture I had when it was one of the children's birthdays or during the loneliness that went with a childless Christmas.

I threw myself into my work but I also played hard and it was rare that I would go back to my home unless I was completely exhausted and ready to fall into my bed. My frustration had already cost me a small fortune in replacing broken furnishings but eventually I would accept that I could not change the situation and had to behave accordingly. My work and my festivals became my release, and even though my children were never far from my thoughts I had come to terms with their absence.

It was cruel, what I had been made to endure, and to this day I still get a great deal of sympathy from my close friends and family who know the circumstances. I had a judge's ruling that I was to be allowed access to my children for three weekends out of every four but, because I could not locate Marion, that ruling would be difficult to implement. I would visit the police station and insist they enforce the ruling, in my favour, but they would have little or no interest in assisting me as they smiled in my face.

I was advised to contact a new group that had been formed called FATHERS FOR JUSTICE but instead I preferred facing my dilemma alone. After all, my life had always been full of issues and life had never seemed to run smoothly.

I would ache and pine for my children like no man ever did, and it would not help that David, the only child I was in contact with, was now having problems of his own due to his recent separation from Nicola and his daughter, Kadi Mae. I did not like what I was hearing because the split had come about due to his excessive drug abuse and I dreaded that he was about to follow my path and press the self-destruct button. I would have many heated arguments with him down the phone but all would be to no avail. I advised him to take note of what had happened to me but I was wasting my breath.

His situation spiralled out of control and even now he has got himself some major problems with some very serious and addictive drugs. We only talk occasionally because, very selfishly, he blames me for a lot of his problems. My son and I used to be very close but he did not appreciate my 'tough love' when I refused to send him any money to fund his habit, and we have not even spoken to each other for a long time now.

I love all four of my children dearly and it pleases me that none of the boys have even been in a courtroom, let alone a prison, and if they have not done by now, at the ages they are, I do not think that is likely to occur. I am aware of this fact because as you will discover in the final chapter, the mystery of my children's whereabouts was about to unfold.

It was not to be a very satisfactory conclusion, but at least minimal contact had taken place. It would be a very big 'kick in the teeth' but wasn't that how my life was meant to be?

CHAPTER 31

My life, by now, should have had some semblance of order to it, considering my age, but I would never be afforded that luxury. I had recently been made redundant from my warehouse position because the company had been bought out and relocated to another area. I had no source of income and my age was against me regarding finding another job. Ageism should not exist but unfortunately it does take place, and I would have the added disadvantage of my hands being emblazoned with tattoos, and the fact that I had a criminal record would never put me in a favourable light.

I applied for a few jobs but I would not even make any shortlist let alone get a foot in the door. To be truthful I had always preferred having a job wherever possible, but if my back was against the wall I would resort to any means at my disposal to earn money.

I had recently met a girl called Joanne and it took me a

while to realise that she was an alcoholic because she would conceal bottles without my knowledge. It was a very volatile relationship in the early days and I had realised it was not for me anymore, but unfortunately I had left it too late as Joanne informed me she was pregnant. It wasn't a planned pregnancy and we had not taken any precautions because she was of the opinion that she was too old. I was now under increased pressure to organise some additional source of income, and so I decided to buy some equipment and begin to cultivate some cannabis plants.

I am a very resourceful character and very quick to learn, and after going through a slight learning curve with a few mistakes, I very soon became adept at producing some very high quality plants that would provide me with a reasonable amount of money with each twelve-week cycle. I had converted one of my bedrooms into a mini greenhouse which no one was allowed to go into and I had some very expensive filter systems to mask and disguise the strong smell of the plants.

For all that, Joanne was pregnant and it should have been a happy period, but that would never be the case as I began to dislike her more and more. I knew she was still drinking, although she would deny it, and it would be the subject of many arguments in the early stages of the pregnancy.

Although I was in my mid-fifties I was quite looking forward to the prospect of being a father again, or maybe I wanted a child to compensate for the fact that my other children were not around. However, fate would deal me a cruel blow and put paid to that when Joanne miscarried the baby in my bathroom, and witnessing this would affect me for a very long time. I could not bear to enter my bathroom for ages afterwards, and preferred using a neighbouring flat to do my washing and toilet duties.

Maybe it was a blessing in disguise because I had long since realised I did not wish to continue the relationship with Joanne, and I soon made this clear to her after we had got over the initial shock of the miscarriage.

It was a very stressful time for me and I would need to resort to being treated by a psychiatrist again as my depression returned with a vengeance. My whole life had always seemed to revolve around a succession of doctors and having therapy but I do not wake up each day and enjoy being depressed. It is an illness that I have to accept is always going to trouble me, and I have to learn this will always be the case.

Joanne had taken the end of our relationship pretty badly and in typical fashion of 'the woman scorned' she set about causing me as many problems as she possibly could. She rang the local police and informed them of my cannabis production, and as I will explain shortly, this would result in an early morning raid involving a great number of police officers accompanied by council officials as I rented the property from the local council. I was placed under arrest for the cultivation of cannabis and the council officer informed me that my tenancy was now terminated and I should hand my keys to him immediately. I was not prepared to accept this to be the case, and after a legal consultation an arrangement was reached with the council to give me a twelve-month probation period as long as I corrected my behaviour.

The police had managed to keep up their record of having detained me in each and every one of the last five decades. I had to admit it was getting just a little embarrassing being placed in handcuffs at the age that I was. I have seen cell blocks change in all sorts of manner.

From my early days of internment, when brutality would be rife, to the present day of one's every single movement monitored by CCTV which thereby ensured that a prisoner's rights were adhered to!!! Obviously most things have changed for the better but I would much rather not be giving my views on custody suites, and I would not even wish to see the inside of one ever again.

A very surprising event took place shortly after I ended my relationship with Joanne. As I had done on so many occasions before, I checked all the voting registers in the local library for Nuneaton and the outlying areas and my heart raced when I noticed the name and address of a certain Troy Ginnelly. I wrote a letter off to the address in Tamworth and although my sister told me not to build my hopes up, in case it was not my son, I was more than a little confident that it must be him. It would be a tense wait while I raced to greet the postman each morning, but finally my son made contact, and after we had managed to meet up I was to discover that I also had another three grandchildren.

The joy I felt was immeasurable at that first meeting, because finally the mystery of my children's whereabouts had come to an end. A great weight was lifted from my shoulders and even though it would not be a completely satisfactory conclusion, I would still be filled with happiness.

By now I had taken to using the internet, and because of this I was able to access both my other son, Kyle, and my daughter, Demi, on the social networking site Facebook, but the exchanges that took place were not exactly music to my ears. Both of them have assured me they want nothing to do with me, and they do not even regard me as a father.

They have no wish to meet me and describe me as being no more than a stranger.

My daughter, Demi, seems to have turned out to be a very bright and pretty girl who has only recently turned eighteen, and I am very proud, although she is insistent that she will never want to meet me.

My other son, Kyle, has also expressed that he has no wish to even have any contact with me and so, yet again, I am left to lick my wounds. However, I know now where they all live and work, but I am a realist and feel it would serve no purpose me showing up on any doorstep or at their place of work. If anything, it would possibly complicate matters more. They are living under a different surname so I feel it is only fair that I honour their wishes and not embarrass or inconvenience them in any way. I now know why I had not been able to trace them all of the years I had been searching.

They had been living under an assumed name and my one piece of good fortune was that Troy had needed to change his surname back to Ginnelly so that he could marry his partner. I have the consolation of having Troy back in my life, and he has proved to be a very loyal and loving son who has a key to my home and is welcome to visit any time he chooses. I am proud that he has allowed me to build the bridges, with him, that I have, and he has done more to raise my spirits than anyone or anything in the past fifteen years.

I love all of my four children equally but I find myself unable to speak to two of them and, as I mentioned, my eldest son, David, has serious drug issues which makes communication difficult. Maybe I have a lot to answer for, and so I have to accept my fate.

Lots of people on my estate will testify that I was a very good father who would take the children everywhere, but it saddens me that I seem to have nothing in my favour in the eyes of the children. All I can do is hope against hope that the views of Kyle and Demi change, but I do not think that is likely to happen. They both seem to be doing well in life and it would not be fair for me to disrupt that in any way. All I can do is wish you both continued success and hope everything bodes well for your futures.

My own life has not been too fortuitous and I have nothing to offer except myself and my love but, seemingly, that is not required, so I just have to bite the bullet and take it on the chin. I have to concentrate on my own life and attempt to turn it around, but I seem to have left it a little late although, at the present time, I have recently met a suitable partner, Angela Sullivan, who intends to ensure that I begin to behave and lead an honest and upstanding existence.

I met 'Angie' through Facebook and it became instantly clear that we had a strong attraction for each other, and I feel that this lady is exactly what I need in my life. It was rather ironic that I have a miniature Jack Russell dog called Stella and Angie has her own dog called Charlie who is also a Jack Russell. It was like a computer dating agency had thrown us together.

Stella and Charlie!!! The two banes of my life, by way of alcohol and drugs. You could not make this shit up!! If I ever walk the dogs down the canal towpath and I need to shout them to come back it has now become a standing joke amongst all of my neighbours that each time I shout the name 'Charlie' I am offering my wares and looking for a drug deal.

I have settled into a routine with Angie and I'm hoping the relationship develops into a long-standing one. As part of the package Angie has a daughter called Bracken who is sixteen years of age and a typical troublesome teenager, and I suppose I will need to be called on to give her the direction in life that I never had the chance to do with my own children. Hopefully this should be the turning point in my life that I have been looking for and it is about time I redirected myself and brought some stability into my home.

David's ex-partner, Nicola, has had two more children who I regard also as my own grandchildren, and now David has re-married in Yorkshire – a nice girl called Vanessa, who also has given me a grandson called Jack.

The roll-call is an ever-increasing one and I now have Kadi, Chloe, Matthew, Dylan, Jack, Josh and baby Grace to keep me busy as a grandad, and Angie also has an extended family. If all of them cannot keep me busy and keep me out of the clutches of the police then I only have myself to blame. I have all of them to sleep on the odd occasion and I operate a rota system regarding taking them on holidays to Butlins in Skegness.

I think our mother would be proud of the legacy she has left behind, because all of her ten children have managed to accumulate in excess of thirty grandchildren, thus ensuring that Nuneaton will be overrun with the family surname for many years to come.

We can only hope it will be for all of the right reasons!

CHAPTER 32

To conclude I would like to offer some sort of apology to anyone that was brutalised at my hands, but I did not come out of it in too good a shape myself. My face is testimony to the fact that I also received far too many beatings. My eyes and mouth carry the scars of many stitched-up wounds. I would also lose my teeth and spend time in hospital because of some wayward snooker ball!

I have had no feeling on the right side of my head for the past thirty years due to a severe beating at the hands of prison warders.

The tendons on my right hand to my thumb and forefinger no longer work because of a broken bottle being stabbed into my wrist.

My ribs were broken by excessive violence, again from prison warders. I could go on forever with my list of injuries but I would just like to point out that I did not set out to live my life that way.

From being a cute little boy dressed in a duffle coat and wellington boots on my feet I became an orphan overnight that nobody seemed to want to foster. That little boy would have conkers and marbles in his pockets, like any other little boy, and perhaps the scariest thing I would ever do is pull out my pet mouse to scare the little girls and make them scream!

I could not even begin to try to determine how I became so violent throughout the years. Would it be inherent? Was I destined to be that way no matter what had occurred to affect me? Or was it exactly how my father had prophesised that I was a 'bad little bastard'? I would like to think that outside influences dictated much of the way I turned out, and although I am not entirely blameless, I would expect a little sympathy.

I intend to settle down and bring all of my criminal activity to a (long overdue) end. The police have locked me up for decade after decade but I have now decided to raise the white flag and call a truce. I can never bring myself to respect anyone in a position of authority because I have very bad memories of my treatment at your hands but I would like this book to cleanse my soul and be a little forgiving for the events that took place.

Along the way I met many people who gave me their own particular direction in life and I thank them all sincerely because, but for them, I could quite easily have fallen into the wrong hands at those moments in time.

The 'traveller' people who taught me the art of squatting and survival on the streets – I can never thank you enough for fostering and adopting me as one of your own.

The West Indian community in Huddersfield who took me under their wing when I did not return to Borstal after a short home-leave period. These people fed me, clothed me and introduced me to 'shabeens' and all that was good in their culture. I spent one of the best summers of my life in their company, and when I finally handed myself into the police and was returned to the borstal, I had many fond memories to comfort me while I, once again, spent my inevitable spell in the solitary confinement block polishing the dust bin to yet another pristine finish. I was given fourteen days in the seclusion block and another fourteen days added on to my sentence as extra punishment for being absent, and because of the pleasure of that summer period I had spent and the many characters I had met, the punishment was very easy to accept.

I have met many people in my life who have given me the morals and principles I carry to this day. Far too many to mention in this book but I am sure many of you who are reading this testimony will realise who you all are.

Lots of people ask if I would like to change anything if I could live it all again, and of course I have things I would do a little differently but, all in all, I have led a very interesting, colourful and eventful life and I have enjoyed and witnessed much more than other people could imagine. Yes, I was perhaps dealt a bad hand, but each and every one of us have things sent to test us and we either sink or swim. If all of our lives panned out the same and without variation then what a boring life we would all lead. It's the twist and turns that give us all the strength to build up our characters to what becomes the finished article. None of us can ever expect to be perfect but I can safely say I have corrected my behaviour to such an extent that I will never see the inside of a penal establishment again.

I have not come out of it unscathed, because I have many psychological problems and need professional counselling on a regular basis, but I have managed to come to terms with much of the drama that life threw at me. It is not a life I would recommend to everyone, but I had to find my feet in life much quicker than most. I lived the high life with vast amounts of money around me and in contrast I now find myself, due to ill-health, struggling by on benefits and left with nothing except my memories to dwell on.

There have been many other stories that could have been told in this book, but from a legal point of view it would be unwise to put them down in print. I have protected the identities of certain people involved in some of the activities, but the majority of us who did the crime would also, unfortunately, have had to serve the time.

We are surrounded by a world full of corrupt politicians and bankers who milk our system to the maximum and who cannot stick their noses deep enough into the trough. At least I like to think I am a likeable rogue, and my principles and standards are now far superior to those of the so-called 'pillars of society'. Obviously some people may disagree and say I got everything I deserved, and I would need to accept that we are all entitled to our own opinions and accept any criticism they may have.

While I wrote this book it opened many old wounds from the skeletons I had long since left in the cupboard, but I felt it was time to tell my story. It cost me yet another relationship along the way because of my continual mood swings whilst I reflected back on my life, but I can readily deal with that because I am quite a complicated character, and if I am to be truthful I believe I am destined to be alone anyway. I spent many years in the solitude of solitary confinement, and to be honest I think I am at my happiest when I am in my own company. I have had to search deep within myself to complete this book and I hope that anyone who knows me personally and who gets a chance to read it still manages to look at me in a favourable light.

If I was to be asked, "Does crime pay?" I would have to say it is possible to enjoy that moment in time when the money and fast cars are readily available, but inevitably it becomes a house of cards waiting to fall over. I never learnt how to drive but my brothers had all the trappings that went with the period and I would accompany them in many expensive makes of transport. None of us are left with much of anything now and I mentioned that I am struggling by on benefits and only my memories for company. I still live with weapons close at hand in every room of my house because that is the mindset this sort of lifestyle leaves you with. Not that I accumulated many enemies along the way. I just sleep sounder with the knowledge that I have things close at hand to protect myself.

All I am left with is a very empty pocket, a succession of failed relationships, and some children in different areas of the country. Yet another relationship broke down while I was writing this story and I would have to be the first to admit I am a complex person and I neither have the patience nor the commitment to make any pairing work.

I have and always will enjoy the company of ladies, but I have reached that stage in life where I am happier in my own company and I have built a brick wall around myself. I am set in my ways and I have come a long way and survived much in my life, but I am finally of the opinion that I can put my criminal career behind me and not have the need to constantly look over my shoulder.

Throughout my life I have met thousands of nice people and I like to think that I am respected by many of you and I have left you all with a favourable impression. I have found myself in some dire situations but I also have many good memories to carry me into my old age and I thank each and every one of you for bringing those memorable moments into my life.

My best wishes go out to you all.

WELLIES AND WARDERS

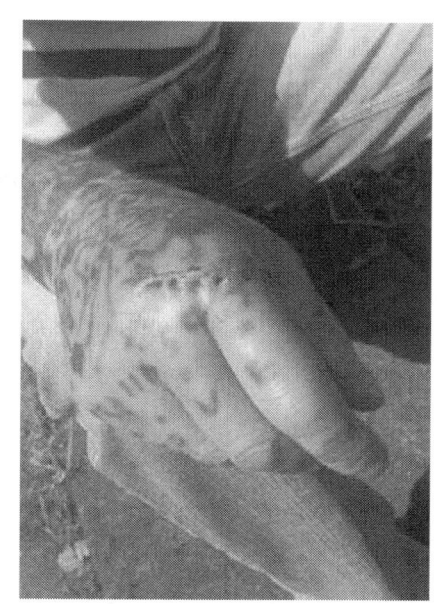

Don't ever punched someones teeth (ouch!)

Football

DAVE GINNELLY

Last Updated: Saturday, 7 May, 2005, 21:42 GMT 22:42 UK

E-mail this to a friend   Printable version

Father-of-three found shot dead

A murder inquiry has been launched after a 48-year-old father-of-three was shot dead in his car in Warwickshire on election day.

James Fenton was shot twice in the head as he pulled up outside his house in Charles Eaton Road, Bedworth, on Thursday night.

James Fenton was found shot dead in his silver Peugeot 206

He was found slumped in his car by a passer-by on Friday morning with the lights on and engine still running.

Police say Mr Fenton's killer laid in wait for him.

Detective Superintendent Ken Lawrence said his death was not a motiveless crime and appealed for information.

"Mr Fenton was not a man with a regular routine - he did not come and go at specific times," he said.

"Therefore, we believe that whoever did this must have been waiting for him outside his home on Thursday night."

Post mortem

The reason for Mr Fenton's murder "remains a mystery", he added.

A post mortem confirmed Mr Fenton had been shot in the head at close range.

Earlier, the area was cordoned off and police officers conducted house to house enquiries.

Mr Fenton was separated from his wife and had lived locally for some years.

His children are aged between 17 and 24.

Irish Jimmy

WELLIES AND WARDERS

Jackie (my second mum)

Gran

Kevin Hanson (killed in Holland)

WELLIES AND WARDERS

Lee Cass and Caron Morton

Nuneaton, England Flag (Europe trip)

Paddy Ginelly (my brother)

WELLIES AND WARDERS

Red Lion Inn

Some top Leeds lads

DAVE GINNELLY

The Donnihorne

The ECLIPSE
LOWER FORD STREET, COVENTRY

WELLIES AND WARDERS

The lads

The Wine Bar

Printed in Great Britain
by Amazon.co.uk, Ltd.,
Marston Gate.